BAUCHER'S

METHOD OF HORSEMANSHIP.

T. Sinclair's Lith.

M[r] BAUCHER,

upon Partisan

A METHOD

OF

HORSEMANSHIP,

FOUNDED UPON NEW PRINCIPLES:

INCLUDING THE

BREAKING AND TRAINING OF HORSES:

WITH

INSTRUCTIONS FOR OBTAINING A GOOD SEAT.

BY F. BAUCHER.

SECOND AMERICAN EDITION,

Revised and corrected from the Ninth Paris Edition.

ILLUSTRATED WITH ENGRAVINGS.

PHILADELPHIA:
A. HART, LATE CAREY AND HART.
1852.

PHILADELPHIA:
T. K. AND P. G. COLLINS, PRINTERS.

TRANSLATOR'S PREFACE.

THE author's introduction to his "Method of Horsemanship" is omitted in this edition, because it contains much that would be uninteresting to the American reader. It mentions the great difficulties he encountered in attracting the attention of the public to his system, and the complete success with which it was crowned when once this attention was attracted.* One paragraph from it,

* The following fact will prove the great popularity of the work: The first edition was published in 1842; in the first year, two editions were published, and since then seven more, making nine editions in eight years.—TRANS. NOTE.

which contains the principle upon which his whole method is founded, is here given:—

"However favored by nature the horse may be, he requires a preparatory exercise to enable his forces to afford each other mutual assistance; without this, everything becomes mechanical and hazardous, as well on his part as on that of the rider.

"What musician could draw melodious sounds from an instrument without having exercised his fingers in handling it? He would certainly, if he attempted such a thing, produce only false, discordant sounds; and the same thing occurs in horsemanship, when we undertake to make a horse execute movements for which he has not been prepared."

M. Baucher presents the official documents upon the subject of the introduction of his method into the French army, with the following introductory remarks:—

"Since the first publication of my method, indisputable facts have attested the truth of the principles therein contained. Field-Marshal the Minister of War has appointed a commission, presided over by Lieutenant-General the Marquis Oudinot, to examine into its advantages.*

"Fifty horses, some from the troop, and others belonging to officers which had not yet commenced their education, or which were considered difficult to manage, or vicious, were subjected to the experiment, which commenced on the 21st March, 1842. The demands of the service of the garrison of Paris permitting only a small number of

* "The commission was composed of Lieut.-General Oudinot, Col. Carrelet, Commander of the Municipal Guard, the Chef d'Escadrons De Novital, commanding the Cavalry Riding-School, and the Captain-instructors de Gués, of the 5th Cuirassiers, and De Mesanges, of the 3d Lancers."

cuirassiers, municipal guards, and first class lancers to be put at the disposition of the commission, nearly all the horses were intrusted to riders who were by no means intelligent, or else whose education was not very much advanced. The riders themselves exercised their horses. On the 9th of April —that is to say, after fifteen lessons—Field-Marshal the Minister of War wished to witness the results of the system which he had ordered to be tried. His excellency was accompanied by the members of the committee of cavalry, and many other general officers. The men being completely armed and equipped, and the horses caparisoned, they executed, individually and in troop, at all the paces, movements that, up to this time, had only been required of horses that had been exercised for five or six months under experienced riders. The Minister of War followed all the trials with the greatest interest, and before retiring expressed his complete satisfaction, and announced his intention of having a general application of it made in the army."

Among the official documents in favor of Baucher's method is a letter from M. Champmontant, Lieutenant-Colonel of the Staff, Secretary of the Committee of Cavalry, in which he requests M. Baucher to fix a convenient time to appear before the committee and explain his system more completely, that they may consider upon its adoption in the army; another from Lieutenant-General Marquis Oudinot to M. Baucher. In this letter, the general informs M. Baucher that the Minister of War has decided that a series of experiments shall be made upon his method of breaking new horses, and such as were considered difficult to manage.

Then follows the report upon the trials of Baucher's method, and a recapitulation of the daily operations, by the *Chef d'Escadrons* de Novital, commanding the Royal School at Saumur. The complete success of the trial is mentioned above, and an extract only from the report will be here given :—

"But it may be objected, will not this species of captivity, to which the new method will subject the horse, prevent his lasting? Will it not be the source of his premature decay? To this it is easy to answer by a comparison, which to us appears conclusive. When all the wheel-work of a machine fits well together, so that each part furnishes its share of action, there is harmony, and consequently need of a less force; so when, in an organized body, we are enabled to obtain suppleness and pliability in all the parts, the equilibrium becomes easy, there is suppleness and lightness, and in consequence a diminution of fatigue.

"Far from injuring the horse, the new

method has the advantage of being a great auxiliary in developing the muscles, particularly in a young subject."

Extract from the report to Lieutenant-General Oudinot, by M. Carrelet, Colonel of the Municipal Guard of Paris:—

"To shorten this narration, I would say that the officers of the Municipal Guard are unanimous in their approval of M. Baucher's proceedings, applied to the breaking of young horses.

"We have assisted at the education of forty troop horses, all more or less difficult to manage; and we are convinced that, by Baucher's system, they have been more advanced in fifteen days than they would have been in six months by the proceedings we have been accustomed to follow.

"I am so convinced of the efficiency of the means practised by M. Baucher, that I am about to subject to them all the horses of my five squadrons."

Extract from the report of Lieutenant-General Marquis Oudinot to his excellency the Marshal the Minister of War:—

"That the system of M. Baucher may produce in the army all the expected advantages, it would be necessary to have a certain number of instructors, initiated in it as completely as possible, that they may be able to teach it afterwards.

"In consequence of which, I have the honor to propose to you to order—

"1st. That upon the return to Saumur of the commanding officer of the riding-school, the young horses be broken after Baucher's method, and observations be made upon the advantages or disadvantages that it presents.

"2d. That in the 5th Cuirassiers and the

3d Lancers, the application of this method be continued.

"3d. That the different bodies of cavalry within a circle of twenty-five leagues around Paris detach, for about two months, their captain-instructor and one officer, who shall come to study the system of M. Baucher."

The Minister of War immediately issued these three orders, and also three additional ones :—

"4th. M. Baucher, Jr. will repair to the camp at Luneville, and sojourn there during the months of June, July, and August. The captain-instructors, and one lieutenant from the troops of horse stationed in the neighborhood of Paris, will be ordered to Luneville during those months to study the Baucher system.

"5th. M. Baucher, Jr. will receive an indemnity of five hundred francs a month.

"6th. Each of the troops of horse and the establishments of unbroken horses will receive two copies of the work entitled 'Method of Horsemanship, founded upon New Principles, by M. Baucher.'"

Extract from the report of the Chef d'Escadrons Grenier, appointed to the command of the officers detached to Paris, by ministerial decision of the 20th May, 1842, to study the method of horsemanship of M. Baucher:—

"The officers detached to Paris were twenty-two in number, the captain-instructor and a lieutenant from each regiment. * * * They exercised for thirty-nine days. * * These officers did not all arrive at Paris with the belief that they could be taught anything. One-half were captain-instructors, the rest lieutenants intended to become the same. Thus, in the beginning, there was very little confidence, on the part of the officers, in their new professor, sometimes even opposition, but always zeal and good-will.

"Little by little, confidence came, and opposition disappeared; but only at the end of the first month, after about twenty-five lessons, did all the officers, without exception, understand the method and recognize the superiority of M. Baucher's principles over those previously known.

"Before leaving, they all approved of the new method, and desired its application in their regiments.

"The method of horsemanship of M. Baucher is positive and rational; it is easy to understand, especially when studied under the direction of some one who knows it. It is attractive to the rider, gives him a taste for horses and horsemanship, tends to develop the horse's qualities, especially that of lightness, which is so delightful to discover in a saddle-horse. * * * Applied to the breaking of young horses, it develops their instinct, makes them find the domination of the rider easy and pleasant; it preserves them from the premature ruin that an improper breaking often brings with it; it may shorten the time devoted to the education of the horse; and it interests the riders employed in it."

M. Desondes, Lieutenant of the 9th Cuirassiers, winds up a long and highly favorable report upon the breaking of young horses for the army with the words, "To Baucher the cavalry is grateful."

Extracts from the sixth and last report upon the trials of the new method of horsemanship of M. Baucher :—

"The first trials are concluded. The principal movements of the platoon-drill on horseback, running at the head and charging, have completed the exercises.

Thus, thirty-five lessons have sufficed to perfect the instruction of the tractable as well as the intractable horses confided to me. The first rough work with the horse —that is to say, the exercises with the snaffle prescribed by the orders—used to take up as much time as this, and then we scarcely dared to touch the curb-rein. In this view, the new system is of great utility for cavalry.

"But the promptness with which we can put new horses in the ranks is not the only advantage the new method presents; it guarantees, besides, the preservation of the horse; it develops his faculties and his powers; these increase by the harmony and proper application of the forces among themselves, and by their rational and opportune use. It is not the immoderate employment of force which conquers a rebellious horse, but the well-combined use of an ordinary force. The Baucher system ought to be considered eminently preservative, since the breaking, being well graduated and well combined, cannot have an injurious influence upon the horse's *physique;* and his forces being at the disposition of the rider, it is he, the absolute dispenser of these forces, who is responsible for their duration or premature destruction. * * * I repeat it, that the new method would be a great benefit, an indisputable improvement for cavalry. * * * I pray then for its adoption, and ardently desire its prompt introduction into the cavalry. (Signed) DE NOVITAL."

Extract from the *Spectateur Militaire:*—

"Passionately fond of a science that, from his childhood, has been the object of studies as productive as they were persevering, M. Baucher, after having obtained from the horse a submission almost magical, is not willing to be the only one who shall profit by his meditations; he has put them cleverly together, and his written method is now in the hands of all those who occupy themselves with horsemanship. * * * The division of dragoons, and the instructors of the different troops of horse that composed a part of the camp of Luneville, intended to execute, after the principles of the new method, and in the presence of their royal highnesses, the Dukes of Orleans and Nemours, equestrian exercises that would have drawn together thousands of spectators. The mournful event that deprived France of the prince royal did not allow of this performance having the *éclat* that was intended. Nevertheless, M. the Duke de Nemours, wishing to judge for himself of the results, has had part of these exercises performed in his presence."

The death of the Duke of Orleans, and

the indifference and afterwards opposition of the Duke de Nemours, were the principal causes that prevented the system of M. Baucher from being adopted for the cavalry of the whole French army. The former was an ardent admirer of the system, while the latter was an equally ardent admirer of a rival professor of horsemanship.

Extract from a letter of M. de Gouy, Colonel of the 1st Hussars, to M. Baucher :—

"So far from the horse's muscular power being lessened by the repetition of the flexions, is it not increased by having all the advantage of exercise over repose, of work over indolence? Does not the muscular system develop itself, physiologically speaking, in proportion to these conditions? Will not address and vigor be the result of these gymnastics? Has the habitual difference between the forces of the right and the left arm any other cause than the difference in the daily use of the one to the prejudice of the other?"

Baucher says: "To prove the complete success of my mission to Saumur, I will back, according to my custom, my assertions by positive facts. The officers present at my course of instruction were seventy-two in number; of these, sixty-nine have sent in reports favorable to my method. There were but *three dissenting voices.*"

This statement is followed by letters from General Prévost, De Novital, &c., all highly commending the system.

Baucher's method has been reprinted in Belgium, and translated into Dutch and German. In the latter language, several different translations have been written, one by M. Ritgen, Lieutenant of the 4th Regiment of *Houlans* (Prussian), and the other by M. de Willisen, Lieutenant-Colonel of the 7th Cuirassiers (Prussian).

The translator will give some extracts from the preface to M. De Willisen's translation, as it shows that some of the difficulties met with by the former were not altogether escaped by his German *confrère*.

"After positive results had proved to me most convincingly that M. Baucher's was the best of all existing methods, I thought that it would be useful to translate it. This translation seemed at first much easier than it proved in the sequel; above all, it was actually impossible for me to render in German, as I wished, such technical French expressions as *attaques*, *acculement*, *assouplissement*, *ramener*, *rassembler*, &c., retaining their clearness and conciseness. In German, I could only find expressions that were incomplete. On this account, I have put all the words, for which I could not find a clear equivalent in German, in the original French.

"Horses may be broken with much success upon other principles—they have been broken before M. Baucher's time—but no work has thrown so much light upon horse education; no other method has taught such simple and sure means, nor presented a like result with the same certainty. He who would ride with safety and satisfaction ought to be completely master of an obedient and correct horse. To obtain this result, M. Baucher gives the surest means, and points out the shortest road.

"The exact knowledge of the obstacles which the horse presents to instruction; the simple manner, easy to understand and easy to execute, of making these obstacles disappear, distinguish this method from all preceding ones, and render it of the greatest importance to all riders.

"The close relations that are established between rider and horse give the former such a certainty of hand and legs, and the latter such suppleness and obedience, that a like result has never previously been obtained.

"Until now, no horseman has ever had such clear and sure means for breaking a horse given to him, even approximatively, as are contained in this book. The trial will give the most convincing proofs of this when we undertake to apply the principles therein contained; but that can only be considered a trial when made by following strictly what is prescribed in the method. There is no other method that can put the horse so certainly under the control of the rider's hand and legs; no other method succeeds in developing so much address and assurance in horse or rider: the horse feels undisturbed, the rider is absolute master of him, and both are at their ease. * * * This new method teaches, further, what is of very great importance, the most certain means of making the rider perfectly in harmony with his horse, so that they can understand and mutually trust one another, in such a way that the horse obeys as punctually as the rider guides him skilfully. In place of being obliged to break every horse after our own particular fashion, we will only, thanks to this method, have to occupy ourselves with one horse, for it teaches us that the same means are applicable to all horses. It is unnecessary to enumerate the advantages which the instruction of the rider gains from it, for he escapes the martyrdom of the lessons being given him on awkward badly-broken horses. Riders will sooner become masters of these managed horses, and will acquire in six weeks a seat that will come of itself, and their touch will be developed much more quickly.

" Finally, men learn very quickly to put

in practice means that are applied on foot, and there is this great advantage in it;—they can see better the moment that the neck becomes flexible and the jaw without contraction: besides this, their hand becomes much more delicate than it would have become in a much greater space of time, if the application had taken place in the saddle.

"Until lately, only men of great talent were able to break horses; now, by practising this new method, which demonstrates clearly the means of breaking, every rider, in a very short time, can acquire the knowledge necessary to render a horse fit for use. * * * A person commencing to learn this method, and who is obliged to work from the book, ought to proceed slowly and cautiously in the application of principles that are not familiar to him. He ought first to endeavor to perfect his seat, his position, his touch, the obedience of his horse, and his paces; he will thus make great progress in the breaking, and be enabled to undertake the application of the new method.

"DE WILLISEN,

"*Lieut.-Col. of the 7th Cuirassiers.*"

M. Baucher received from the King of Prussia a magnificent snuff box of elegantly carved gold, as a token of the satisfaction of his majesty with our author's system.

In consequence of the opposition mentioned above, Baucher's system was discontinued in the French army, in spite of the almost unanimous wish of the officers. But he has gained a name as the first horseman of this or any other age—the first who could not only manage horses himself, but teach others to do so equally well. This has been proved under the translator's own eyes.

A gentleman of this city purchased a

horse, four years old, long, *gangling*, ewe-necked; such a brute as no one but a confident disciple of Baucher would have had anything to do with. Had he hunted the country for a horse with but one merit, that of soundness, and possessing that only because nothing had ever been done to injure it, he could not have been better suited. It was painful to see a good rider in such a quandary as he appeared when mounted upon this animal; but a quiet, confident smile showed what was intended to come of it.

In six weeks from that time, without the horse ever having crossed the threshold of the stable-yard, the writer saw him with his neck arched like the steed in Holy Writ, his haunches well under him, obedient to the lightest touch of hand or heel, ready to do anything that was demanded of him, because he had been put in a position that enabled him to do it.

Since that time, the same person has broken two other horses of greater natural capabilities, and the success was proportionately greater.

Every one who takes any interest in horses, recollects the horse May-Fly, when first introduced to an American audience, by Sands, of Welsh's circus. This horse, a thorough-bred, belonging to the racing stud of Baron Rothschild, was so vicious that he had to be brought upon the race-course in a van, so that he could see nothing till the moment to start arrived. With even this and similar precautions, he was considered dangerous and unmanageable. The master hand was required, and, under its influence, all such things as vice and unmanageable temper disappeared. Instead of violent force on the part of man, which would only have produced more violent force on the part of the brute, Baucher sought out the sources of these resistances, and conquered them in detail.

Is it not worth a few weeks' pleasant labor with your horse to be able to make him move with the grace, elegance, and majesty of this one, or of those we have since seen ridden by Derious, and that French Amazon, Caroline Loyo? It is within the power of every one to do this to a certain extent; and as the education of the rider advances progressively with that of the horse, there are, as Baucher himself says, no limits to the progress of horsemanship, and no performance, *equestrianly* possible, which a horseman, who will properly apply these principles, cannot make his horse execute.

BAUCHER'S

METHOD OF HORSEMANSHIP,

FOUNDED ON NEW PRINCIPLES.

I.

NEW MEANS OF OBTAINING A GOOD SEAT.

It may undoubtedly be thought astonishing that, in the first editions of this work, which had for its object the horse's education, I should not have commenced by speaking of the rider's seat. In fact, this, so important a part of horsemanship, has always been the basis of classical works on the subject. Nevertheless, it is not without a motive that I have deferred treating of this question until now. Had I had nothing new to say on this subject, I might very easily have managed, by consulting old authors, by transposing a sentence here, and changing a word there, to have sent forth into the equestrian world another inutility. But I had other ideas; I wished to make a thorough reform. My system for giving a good seat to the rider, being also an innovation, I feared lest so many new things at one time should alarm even the best-intentioned amateurs, and give a hold to my adversaries. They would not have failed to say that my means of managing a horse were impracticable, or that they could not be applied without recourse to a seat still more impracticable. But now I have proved the contrary—that, upon my plan, horses have been broken by troops without regard to the men's seat. To give more force to my method, and render it more easily comprehensible, I have divested it of all accessories, and said nothing about those new principles that concern the rider's seat. I reserved these last until after the indisputable success of the official trials. By means of these principles, added to those which I have published upon the art of horse-breaking, I shorten the man's work, and establish a system not only precise, but complete in these two important parts of horsemanship, hitherto so confused.

By following my new instructions relating to the man's seat on horseback, we will promptly arrive at a certain result; they are as easy to understand as to demonstrate. Two sentences are sufficient to explain all to the rider, and enable him to obtain a good seat by the simple advice of the instructor.

The seat of the rider.—The rider will expand his chest as much as possible, so that each part of his body rests upon that next below it, for the purpose of increasing the adhesion of his buttocks to the saddle; the arms will fall easily by the sides. The thighs and legs must, by their own strength, find as many points of contact as possible with the saddle and the horse's sides; the feet will naturally follow the motion of the legs.

You see by these few lines how simple is the rider's seat.

The means which I point out for quickly obtaining a good seat remove all the difficulties which the plan pursued by our predecessors presented. The pupil used to understand nothing of the long catechism, recited in a loud voice by the instructor, from the first word to the last, consequently he could not execute it. Here one word replaces all those sentences; but we previously go through a course of supplings. This course will make the rider expert, and consequently intelligent. One month will not elapse without the most stupid and awkward recruit being able to seat himself properly without the aid of the word of command.

Preparatory lesson (*the lesson to last an hour, two lessons daily for a month*).—The horse is led upon the ground, saddled and bridled. The instructor must take two pupils; one will hold the horse by the bridle, and observe what the other does, that he may be able to perform in his turn. The pupil will approach the horse's shoulder and prepare to mount; for this purpose he will lay hold of and separate with the right hand, a handful of mane, and pass it into the left hand, taking hold as near the roots as possible, without twisting them; he will seize the pommel of the saddle with the right hand, the four fingers inside, and the thumb outside; then springing lightly, he will raise himself upon his wrists. As soon as his middle reaches the height of the horse's withers, he will pass the right leg over the croup, without touching it, and place himself lightly in the saddle. This vaulting will tend to make the man active; and he should be made to repeat it eight or ten times, before letting him finally seat himself. The repetition of this exercise will soon teach him the use of his arms and loins.

Exercise in the saddle.—(This is a stationary exercise on horseback; an old, quiet horse to be chosen in preference; the reins to be knotted, and to hang on his neck.)—The pupil being on horseback, the instructor will examine his natural position, in order to exercise more frequently those parts which have a tendency to give way or stiffen. The lesson will commence with the chest. He must expand the chest, and hold himself in this position for some time, without regard to the stiffness which it will occasion at first. It is by the exertion of force that the pupil will become supple, and not by the *abandon* so much and so uselessly recommended. A movement at first obtained by great effort, will not require so much force after a while, for he will then have gained skill, and skill, in this case, is but the result of exertions properly combined and employed. What is first done with twenty pounds of force reduces itself afterwards to fourteen, to ten, to four. Skill will be the exertion reduced to four pounds. If we commenced by a less, we would not attain this result. The flexions of the loins will be repeated, allowing the pupil often to let himself down into his natural relaxed position, in order to accustom him to throw his chest quickly into a good position. The body being well placed, the instructor will pass: 1st. To the lesson of the arm, which consists in moving it in every direction, first bent, and afterwards extended; 2d. To that of the head; this must be turned right and left without its motions reacting on the shoulders.

When the lessons of the chest, arms, and head give a satisfactory result, which ought to be at the end of four days (eight lessons), we will then pass to the pupil's legs.

He will remove one of his thighs as far as possible from the quarters of the saddle; and afterwards replace it with a rotatory movement from without inwards, in order to make it adhere to the saddle by as many points of contact as possible. The instructor will watch that the thigh does not fall back heavily; it should resume its position by a slowly progressive motion, and without a jerk. He ought, moreover, during the first lesson, to take hold of the pupil's leg, and direct it, to make him understand the proper way of performing this displacement. He will thus save him fatigue, and obtain the result more quickly.

This kind of exercise, very fatiguing at first, requires frequent rests; it would be wrong to prolong the exercise beyond the powers of the pupil. The motions of drawing in (*adduction*, which makes the thigh adhere to the saddle), and putting out (*abduction*, which separates it from the saddle), becoming more easy, the thighs will have acquired a suppleness which will admit of their adhesion to the saddle in a good position. Then comes the flexion of the legs.

Flexion of the legs.—The instructor will watch that the knees always preserve their perfect adherence to the saddle. The legs will be swung backward and forward like the pendulum of a clock; that is, the pupil will raise them so as to touch the cantle of the saddle with his heels. The repetition of these flexions will soon render the legs supple, pliable, and independent of the thighs. The flexions of the legs and thighs will be continued for four days (eight lessons). To make each of these movements more correct and easy, eight days (or sixteen lessons) will be devoted to them. The fifteen days (thirty lessons), which remain to complete the month, will continue to be occupied by the exercise of stationary supplings; but, in order that the pupil may learn to combine the strength of his arms, and that of his loins, he will be made to hold at arm's length, progressively, weights of from ten to forty pounds. This exercise will be commenced in the least fatiguing position, the arm being bent, and the hand near the shoulder, and this flexion will be continued to the full extent of the arm. The chest should not be affected by this exercise, but be kept steady in the same position.

Of the knees.—The strength of pressure of the knees will be judged of, and even obtained, by the aid of the following method: this, which at first sight will perhaps appear of slight importance, will, nevertheless, bring about great results. The instructor will take a narrow piece of leather about twenty inches long; he will place one end of this strap between the pupil's knee and the side of the saddle. The pupil will make use of the force of his knees to prevent its slipping, while the instructor will draw it towards him slowly and progressively. This process will serve as a dynamometer to judge of the increase of power.

The strictest watch must be kept that each force which acts separately does not put other forces in action, that is to say, that the movement of the arms does not influence the shoulders; it should be the same with the thighs, with respect to the body; the legs, with respect to the thighs, &c. &c. The displacement and suppling of each part separately being obtained, the chest and seat will be temporarily displaced, in order to teach the rider to recover his proper position without assistance. This will be done as follows: the instructor, being placed on one side, will push the pupil's hip, so that his seat will be moved out of the seat of the saddle. The instructor will then allow him to get back into the saddle, being careful to watch that, in regaining his seat, he makes use of his hips and knees only, in order to make him use only those parts nearest to his seat. In fact, the aid of the shoulders would soon affect the hand, and this the horse; the assistance of the legs would have still worse results. In a word, in all the displacements, the pupil must be taught not to have recourse, in order to direct the horse, to the means which keep him in his seat, and *vice versâ*, not to employ, in order to keep his seat, those means which direct the horse.

Here but a month has elapsed, and these equestrian gymnastics have made a rider of a person, who at first may have appeared the most unfit for it. Having mastered the preliminary trials, he will impatiently await the first movements of the horse, to give himself up to them with the ease of an experienced rider.

Fifteen days (thirty lessons) will be devoted to the walk, the trot, and the gallop. Here the pupil should solely endeavor to follow the movements of the horse; therefore, the instructor will oblige him to occupy himself only with his seat, and not attempt to guide the horse. He will only exact that the pupil ride at first, straight before him, then in every direction, one rein of the snaffle in each hand. At the end of four days (eight lessons), he may be made to take the curb rein in his left hand. The right hand, which is now free, must be held along-side of the left, that he may early get the habit of sitting square (with his shoulders on a level) ; the horse will trot equally to the right and to the left. When the seat is firmly settled at all the different paces, the instructor will explain simply, the connection between the wrists and the legs, as well as their separate effects.

Education of the horse.—Here the rider will commence the horse's education, by following the progression I have pointed out, and which will be found farther on. The pupil will be made to understand all that there is rational in it, and what an intimate connection exists between the education of the man and that of the horse.

Recapitulation and progression.—

	Days.	Lessons.
1. Flexion of the loins to expand the chest	4	8
2. Extending and replacing of the thighs, and flexion of the legs	4	8
3. General exercise of all the parts in succession	8	16
4. Displacement of the man's body, exercise of the knees, and arms with weights in the hands	15	30
5. Position of the rider, the horse being at a walk, a trot, and a gallop, in order to fashion and settle the seat at these different paces	15	30
6. Education of the horse by the rider	75	150
Total	121	242

II.

OF THE FORCES OF THE HORSE.

Of their causes and effects.—The horse, like all organized beings, is possessed of a weight and a force peculiar to himself. The weight inherent to the material of which the animal is composed, renders the mass inert, and tends to fix it to the ground. The force, on the contrary, by the faculty it gives him of moving this weight, of dividing it, of transferring it from one of his parts to another, communicates movement to his whole being, determines his equilibrium, speed, and direction. To make this truth more evident, let us suppose a horse in repose. His body will be in perfect equilibrium, if each of its members supports exactly that part of the weight which devolves upon it in this position. If he wishes to move forward at a walk, he must transfer that part of the weight, resting on the leg which he moves first, to those that will remain fixed to the ground. It will be the same thing in other paces, the transfer acting from one diagonal to the other in the trot, from the front to the rear, and reciprocally, in the gallop. We must not then confound the weight with the force; the latter determines, the former is subordinate to it. It is by carrying the weight from one extremity to the other that the force puts them in motion, or makes them stationary. The slowness or quickness of the transfers fixes the different paces, which are correct or false, even or uneven, according as these transfers are executed with correctness or irregularity.

It is understood that this motive power is subdivided *ad infinitum,* since it is spread over all the muscles of the animal. When the latter himself determines the use of them, the forces are instinctive; I call them transmitted when they emanate from the rider. In the first case, the man governed by his horse remains the plaything of his caprices; in the second, on the contrary, he makes him a docile instrument, submissive to all the impulses of his will. The horse, then, from the moment he is mounted, should only act by transmitted forces. The invariable application of this principle constitutes the true talent of the horseman.

But such a result cannot be attained instantaneously. The young horse, in freedom, having been accustomed to regulate his own movements, will, at first, submit with difficulty to the strange influence that comes to take the entire control of them. A struggle necessarily ensues between the horse and his rider, who will be overcome unless he is possessed of energy, patience, and, above all, the knowledge necessary to gain his point. The forces of the animal being the element upon which the rider must principally work, first to conquer, and finally to direct them, it is necessary he should fix his attention upon these before anything else. He will study what they are, whence they spring, the parts where they contract the most for resistance, and the physical causes which occasion these contractions. When this is discovered, he will proceed with his pupil by means in accordance with his nature, and his progress will then be rapid.

Unfortunately, we search in vain, in ancient or modern authors on horsemanship, I will not say for rational principles, but even for any data in connection with the forces of the horse. All speak very prettily about resistances, oppositions, lightness, and equilibrium; but none of them have known how to tell us what causes these resistances, how we can combat them, destroy them, and obtain this lightness and equilibrium they so earnestly recommend. It is this gap that has caused the great doubts and obscurity about the principles of horsemanship; it is this that has made the art stationary so long a time; it is this gap, I think, that I am able to fill up.

And first, I lay down the principle that all the resistances of young horses spring, in the first place, from a physical cause, and that this cause only becomes a moral one by the awkwardness, ignorance, and brutality of the rider. In fact, besides the natural stiffness peculiar to all horses, each of them has a peculiar conformation, the greater or less perfection of which constitutes the degree of harmony that exists between the forces and the weight. The want of this harmony occasions the ungracefulness of their paces, the difficulty of their movements, in a word, all the obstacles to a good education. In a state of freedom, whatever may be the bad structure of the horse, instinct is sufficient to enable him to make such a use of his forces as to maintain his equilibrium; but there are movements which it is impossible for him to make, until a preparatory exercise shall have put him in the way of supplying the defects of his organization by a better combined use of his motive power. A horse puts himself in motion only in consequence of a given position; if his forces are such as to oppose themselves to this position, they must first be annulled, in order to replace them by the only ones which can lead to it.

Now, I ask, if, before overcoming these first obstacles, the rider adds to them the weight of his own body, and his unreasonable demands, will not the animal experience still greater difficulty in executing certain movements? The efforts we make to compel him to submission, being contrary to his nature, will we not find in it an insurmountable obstacle? He will naturally resist, and with so much the more advantage, because the bad distribution of his forces will be sufficient to paralyze the efforts of his rider. The resistance then emanates, in this case, from a physical cause: which becomes a moral one from the moment when —the struggle going on with the same processes—the horse begins of his own accord to combine means of resisting the torture imposed on him, and when we undertake to force into operation parts which have not previously been suppled.

When things get into this state, they can only grow worse. The rider, soon disgusted with the impotence of his efforts, will cast back upon the horse the responsibility of his own ignorance; he will brand as a jade an animal possessing the most brilliant resources, and of whom, with more discernment and tact, he could have made a hackney as docile in character, as graceful and agreeable in his paces. I have often remarked that horses considered indomitable are those which develop the most energy and vigor, when we know how to remedy those physical defects which prevent their making use of them. As to those which, in spite of their bad formation, are by a similar system made to show a semblance of obedience, we need thank nothing but the softness of their natures. If they can be made to submit to the simplest exercises, it is only on condition that we do not demand anything more of them; for they would soon find energy to resist any further attempts. The rider can make them go along at different paces to be sure; but how disconnected, how stiff, how ungraceful in their movements, and how ridiculous such steeds make their unfortunate riders look, as they toss them about at will, instead of being guided by them! This state of things is all perfectly natural, unless we destroy the first cause of it: *the bad distribution of their forces, and the stiffness caused by a bad conformation.*

But, it is objected, since you allow that these difficulties are caused by the formation of the horse, how is it possible to remedy them? You do not possibly pretend to change the structure of the animal, and reform the work of nature? Undoubtedly not; but while I confess that it is impossible to give more breadth to a narrow chest, to lengthen too short a neck, to lower too high a croup, to shorten and fill out long, weak, narrow loins, I do not the less insist that, if I prevent the different contractions occasioned by these physical defects, if I supple the muscles, if I make myself master of the forces so as to use them at will, it will be easy for me to prevent these resistances, to give more action to the weak parts, and to moderate those that are too vigorous, and thus make up for the deficiencies of nature.

Such results, I do not hesitate to say, were and still are forever denied to the old methods. But if the science of those who follow the old beaten track finds so constant an obstacle in the great number of horses of defective formation, there are, unfortunately, some horses who, by the perfection of their organization, and the consequent facility of their education, contribute greatly to perpetuate the impotent routines that have been so unfavorable to the progress of horsemanship. A well constituted horse is one, all of whose parts being regularly harmonized, induce the perfect equilibrium of the whole. It would be as difficult for such a subject to leave this natural equilibrium, and take up an improper position, for the purpose of resistance, as it is at first painful for the badly formed horse to come into that just distribution of forces, without which no regularity of movement can be hoped for.

It is then only in the education of these last that the real difficulties of horsemanship consist. With the others the breaking ought to be, so to say, instantaneous; since, all the springs being in their places, there is nothing to be done but to put them in motion; this result is always obtained by my method. Yet the old principles demand two or three years to reach this point. And when, by feeling his way without any certainty of success, the horseman, gifted with some tact and experience, ends by accustoming the horse to obey the impressions communicated to him, the rider imagines that he has surmounted great difficulties, and attributes to his skill a state so near to that of nature, that correct principles would have obtained it in a few days. Then as the animal continues to display in all his movements the grace and lightness natural to his beautiful formation, the rider does not scruple to take all the merit to himself; thus showing himself as presumptuous in this case, as he was unjust when he made the badly formed horse responsible for the failure of his attempts.

If we once admit these truths :—

That the education of the horse consists in the complete subjection of his powers ;

That we can only make use of his powers at will, by annulling all resistances ;

And that these resistances have their

source in the contractions occasioned by physical defects;

The only thing will be to seek out the parts where these contractions operate, in order to endeavor to oppose and destroy them.

Long and conscientious observations have shown me that, whatever be the fault of formation that prevents a just distribution of forces in the horse, it is always in the neck that the most immediate effect is felt. There is no improper movement, no resistance that is not preceded by the contraction of this part of the animal; and as the jaw is intimately connected with the neck, the stiffness of the one is instantly communicated to the other. These two points are the prop upon which the horse rests, in order to annul all the rider's efforts. We can easily conceive the immense obstacle they must present to the impulsions of the latter, since the neck and head being the two principal levers by which we direct the animal, it is impossible to obtain anything from him until we are master of these first and indispensable means of action. Behind, the parts where the forces contract the most for resistance, are the loins and the croup (the haunches).

The contractions of these two opposite extremities are, mutually the one to the other, causes and effects, that is to say, the stiffness of the neck induces that of the haunches, and reciprocally. We can combat the one by the other; and as soon as we have succeeded in annulling them, as soon as we have re-established the equilibrium and harmony that they prevented between the fore and the hind parts, the education of the horse will be half finished. I will now point out the means of infallibly arriving at this result.

III.

THE SUPPLINGS.

THIS work being an exposition of a method which upsets most of the old principles of horsemanship, it is understood that I only address men already conversant with the art, and who join to an assured seat a familiarity with the horse, sufficiently great to understand all that concerns his mechanism. I will not, then, revert to the elementary processes; it is for the instructor to judge if his pupil possess a proper degree of solidity of seat, and is sufficiently a part of the horse; for at the same time that a good seat produces this identification, it favors the easy and regular play of the rider's extremities.

My present object is to treat principally

of the education of the horse; but this education is too intimately bound up in that of the rider, for him to make much progress in the one without a knowledge of the other. In explaining the processes which should produce perfection in the animal, I shall necessarily teach the horseman to apply them himself; he will only have to practice to-morrow what I teach him to-day. Nevertheless, there is one thing that no precept can give; that is, a fineness of touch, a delicacy of equestrian feeling that belongs only to certain privileged organizations, and without which, we seek in vain to pass certain limits. Having said this, we will return to our subject.

We now know which are the parts of the horse that contract the most in resistances, and we feel the necessity of suppling them. Shall we then seek to attack, exercise, and conquer them all at once? No;

this would be to fall back into the old error, the inefficiency of which we are convinced of. The animal's muscular power is infinitely superior to ours; his instinctive forces, moreover, being able to sustain themselves the one by the others, we will inevitably be conquered if we set them in motion all at once. Since the contractions have their seat in separate parts, let us profit by this division to combat them separately, as a skilful general destroys, in detail, forces which, when together, he would be unable to resist.

For the rest, whatever the age, the disposition, and the structure of my pupil, my course of proceeding at the start will always be the same. The results will only be more or less prompt and easy, according to the degree of perfection in his nature, and the influence of the hand to which he has been previously subjected. The suppling, which will have no other object in the case of a well made horse than that of preparing his forces to yield to our impulsions, will re-establish calm and confidence in a horse that has been badly handled; and in a defective formation will make those contractions disappear, which are the causes of resistances, and the only obstacles to a perfect equilibrium. The difficulties to be surmounted will be in proportion to this complication of obstacles, but will quickly disappear with a little perseverance on our part. In the progression we are about to pursue, in order to subject the different parts of the animal to suppling, we will naturally commence with the most important parts, that is to say, with the jaw and the neck.

The head and neck of the horse are at once the rudder and compass of the rider. By them he directs the animal; by them, also, he can judge of the regularity and precision of his movements. The equilibrium of the whole body is perfect, and its lightness complete, when the head and neck remain of themselves easy, pliable, and graceful. On the contrary, there can be no elegance, no ease of the whole, when these two parts are stiff. Preceding the body of the horse in all its impulsions, they ought to give warning, and show by their attitude the positions to be taken, and the movements to be executed. The rider has no power so long as they remain contracted and rebellious; he disposes of the animal at will, when once they are flexible and easily handled. If the head and neck do not first commence the changes of direction, if in circular movements they are not inclined in a curved line, if in backing they do not bend back upon themselves, and if their lightness is not always in harmony with the different paces at which we wish to go, the horse will be free to execute these movements or not, since he will remain master of the employment of his own forces.

From the time I first noticed the powerful influence that the stiffness of the neck exercises on the whole mechanism of the horse, I attentively sought the means to remedy it. The resistances to the hand are always either sideways, upward or downward. I at first considered the neck alone as the source of these resistances, and exercised myself in suppling the animal by flexions, repeated in every direction. The result was immense; but although, at the end of a certain time, the supplings of the neck rendered me perfectly master of the forces of the fore-parts of the horse, I still felt a slight resistance which I could not at first account for. At last, I discovered that it proceeded from the jaw. The flexibility I had communicated to the neck even aided

7

this stiffness of the muscles of the lower jaw, by permitting the horse in certain cases to escape the action of the bit. I then bethought me of the means of combating these resistances in this, their last stronghold, and from that time, it is there that I always commence my work of suppling.

First exercise on foot.—Means of making the horse come to the man, of making him steady to mount, &c. &c.

Before commencing the exercises of flexions, it is essential to give the horse a first lesson of subjection, and teach him to recognize the power of man. This first act of submission, which might appear unimportant, will have the effect of quickly rendering him calm, of giving him confidence, and of repressing all those movements which might distract his attention, and mar the success of the commencement of his education.

Two lessons, of a half hour each, will suffice to obtain the preparatory obedience of every horse. The pleasure we experience in thus playing with him will naturally lead the rider to continue this exercise for a few moments each day, and make it both instructive to the horse and useful to himself. The mode of proceeding is as follows: The rider will approach the horse, without roughness or timidity, his whip under his arm; he will speak to him without raising the voice too much, and will pat him on the face and neck; then with the left hand he will lay hold of the curb reins, about six or seven inches from the branches of the bit, keeping his wrist stiff, so as to present as much force as possible when the horse resists. The whip will be held firmly in the right hand, the point towards the ground, then slowly raised as high as the horse's chest, in order to tap it at intervals of a second. The first natural movement of the horse will be to withdraw from the direction in which the pain comes, by backing away from it. The rider will follow this backward movement, without discontinuing the firm tension of the reins, or the little taps with the whip on the breast, applying them all the time with the same degree of intensity. The rider should be perfectly self-possessed, that there may be no indication of anger or weakness in his motions or looks. Becoming tired of this constraint, the horse will soon seek to avoid the infliction by another movement, and by coming forward he will arrive at it; the rider will seize this second instinctive movement to stop and caress the animal with his hand and voice. The repetition of this exercise will give the most surprising results, even in the first lesson. The horse, having discovered and understood the means by which he can avoid the pain, will not wait till the whip touches him, he will anticipate it by rushing forward at the least gesture. The rider will take advantage of this to effect, by a downward force of the bridle hand, the depression of the neck, and the getting him in hand; he will thus early dispose the horse for the exercises that are to follow.

This training, besides being a great recreation, will serve to make the horse steady to mount, will greatly abridge his education, and accelerate the development of his intelligence. Should the horse by reason of his restless or wild nature become very unruly, we should have recourse to the cavesson, as a means of repressing his disorderly movements, and use it with little jerks. I would add that it requires great prudence and discernment to use it with tact and moderation.

Flexion of the jaw.—The flexions of the jaw, as well as the two flexions of the neck which follow, are executed standing still, the man on foot. The horse will be led on the ground saddled and bridled, the reins on his neck. The man will first see that the bit is properly placed in the horse's mouth, and that the curb-chain is fastened so that he can introduce his finger between the links and the horse's chin. Then looking the animal good-naturedly in the eyes, he will place himself before him near his head, holding his body straight and firm, his feet a little apart to steady himself, and enable him to struggle with advantage against all resistances.*

* I have divided all the flexions into two parts, and, in order to facilitate the understanding of the text, I have added to it plates representing the position of the horse at the moment the flexion is about to commence, and at the moment it is terminated.

1. In order to execute the flexion to the right, the man will take hold of the right curb-rein with the right hand, at about six inches from the branch of the bit, and the left rein with the left hand, at only three inches from the left branch. He will then draw his right hand towards his body, pushing out his left hand so as to turn the bit in the horse's mouth. The force employed ought to be entirely determined by and proportioned to the resistance of the jaw and neck only, so as not to affect the rest of his body. If the horse back, to avoid the flexion, the opposition of the hands should still be continued. If the preceding exercise has been completely and carefully practised, it will be easy by the aid of the whip to prevent this retrograde movement, which is a great obstacle to all kinds of flexions of the jaw and neck. (Plate I.)

2. As soon as the flexion is obtained,

the left hand will let the left rein slip to the same length as the right, then drawing the two reins equally, will bring the head near to the breast, and hold it there oblique and perpendicular, until it sustains itself without assistance in this position. The horse, by champing the bit, will show that he is in hand as well as perfectly submissive. The man, to reward him, will cease drawing on the reins immediately, and after some seconds will allow him to resume his natural position. (Plate II.)

The flexion of the jaw to the left is executed upon the same principles, and by inverse means; the man being carefully to pass alternately from the one to the other.

The importance of these flexions of the jaw is easily understood. The result of them is to prepare the horse to yield instantly to the lightest pressure of the bit, and to supple directly the muscles that join

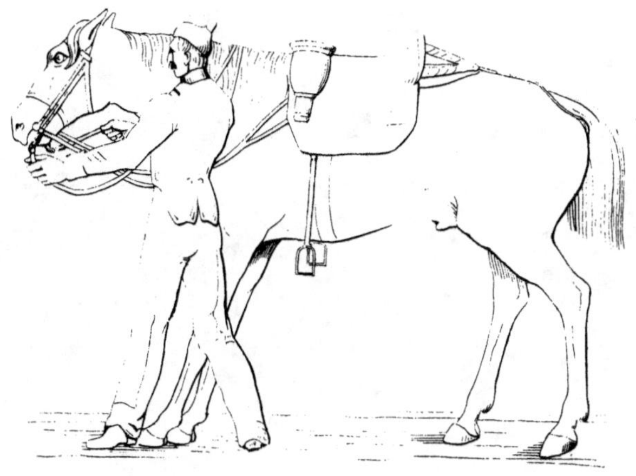

PL. 1

PL. 2

the head to the neck. As the head ought to precede and determine the different attitudes of the neck, it is indispensable that the latter part be always in subjection to the former, and respond to its impulsions. That would be only partially the case, should we obtain the flexibility of the neck alone, which would then make the head obey it, by drawing the latter along in its movements. You see then why, at first, I experienced resistances, in spite of the pliability of the neck, of which I could not imagine the cause. The followers of my method, to whom I have not yet had an opportunity of making known the new means just explained, will learn with pleasure that this process not only brings the flexibility of the neck to a greater degree of perfection, but saves much time in finishing the suppling. The exercise of the jaw, while fashioning the mouth and head, brings along with it the flexion of the neck, and accelerates the getting of the horse in hand.

This exercise is the first of our attempts to accustom the forces of the horse to yield to ours. It is necessary then to manage it very nicely, so as not to discourage him at first. To enter on the flexion roughly would be to shock the animal's intelligence, who would not have had time to comprehend what was required of him. The opposition of the hands will be commenced gently but firmly, nor cease until perfect obedience is obtained; except, indeed, the horse back against a wall, or into a corner; but it will diminish or increase its effect in proportion to the resistance, in a way always to govern it, but not with too great violence. The horse that, at first, will perhaps submit with difficulty, will end by regarding the man's hand as an irresistible regulator, and will become so used to obeying it, that we will soon obtain, by a simple pressure of the rein, what at first required the whole strength of our arms.

At each renewal of the lateral flexions, some progress will be made in the obedience of the horse. As soon as his first resistances are a little diminished, we will pass to the perpendicular flexions or depression of the neck.

Depression of the neck by the direct flexion of the jaw.—1. The man will place himself as for the lateral flexions of the jaw; he will take hold of the reins of the snaffle with the left hand, at six inches from the rings, and the curb-reins at about two inches from the bit. He will oppose the two hands by effecting the depression with the left and the proper position with the right. (Plate III.)

2. As soon as the horse's head shall fall

of its own accord, and by its own weight, the man will instantly cease all kind of force, and allow the animal to resume his natural position. (Plate IV.)

This exercise, being often repeated, will soon supple the elevating muscles of the neck, which play a prominent part in the resistances of the horse, and will besides facilitate the direct flexions and the getting the head in position, which should follow the lateral flexions. The man can execute this, as well as the preceding exercise, by himself; yet it would be well to put a second person in the saddle, in order to accustom the horse to the exercise of the supplings with a rider. This rider should just hold the snaffle-reins, without drawing on them, in his right hand, the nails downward.

The flexions of the jaw have already communicated suppleness to the upper part of the neck, but we have obtained it by

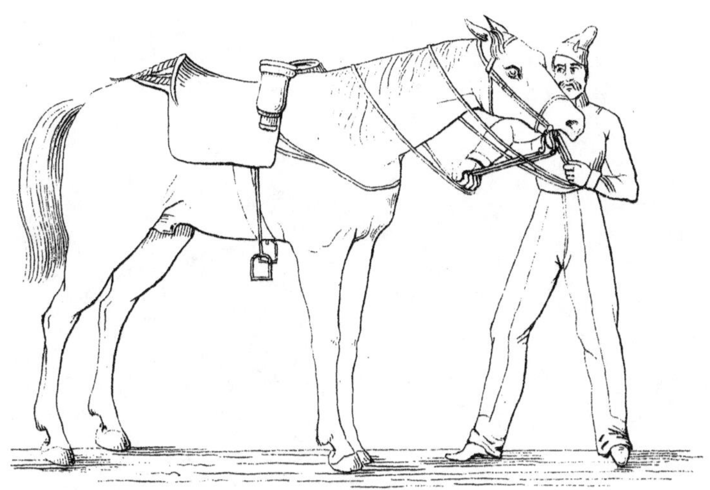

PL. 3.

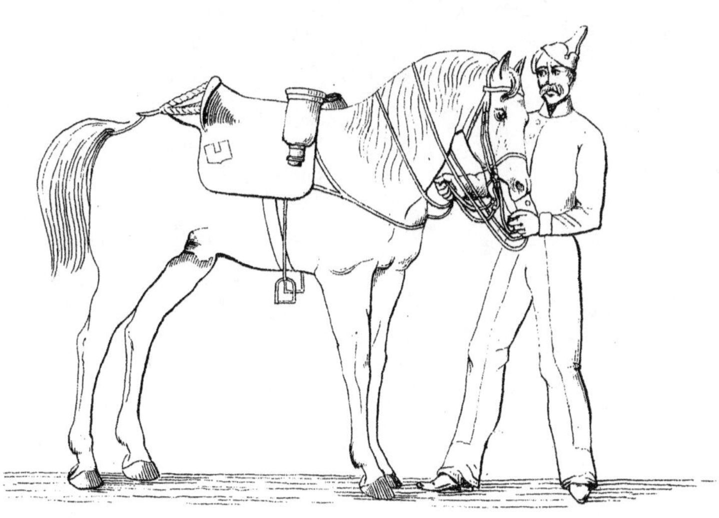

PL. 4

Sinclairs Lith.

means of a powerful and direct motive power, and we must accustom the horse to yield to a less direct regulating force. Besides, it is important that the pliability and flexibility, especially necessary in the upper part of the neck, should be transmitted throughout its whole extent, so as to destroy its stiffness entirely.

The force from above downward, practised with the snaffle, acting only by the head-stall on the top of the head, often takes too long to make the horse lower his head. In this case, we must cross the two snaffle-reins by taking the left rein in the right, and the right rein in the left hand, about six or seven inches from the horse's mouth, in such a way as to cause a pretty strong pressure upon the chin. This force, like all the others, must be continued until the horse yields. The flexions being repeated with this more powerful agent, will put him in a condition to respond to the means previously indicated. If the horse responded to the first flexions represented by Plate IV., it would be unnecessary to make use of this one. (Plate V.)

We can act directly on the jaw so as to render it prompt in moving. To do this, we take the left curb-rein about six inches from the horse's mouth, and draw it straight towards the left shoulder; at the same time draw the left rein of the snaffle forward, in such a way that the wrists of the person holding the two reins shall be opposite and on a level with each other. The two opposed forces will soon cause a separation of the jaws, and end all resistance. The force ought always to be proportioned to that of the horse, whether in his resistance, or in his lightness. Thus, by means of this direct force, a few lessons will be sufficient to give a pliability to the part in question which

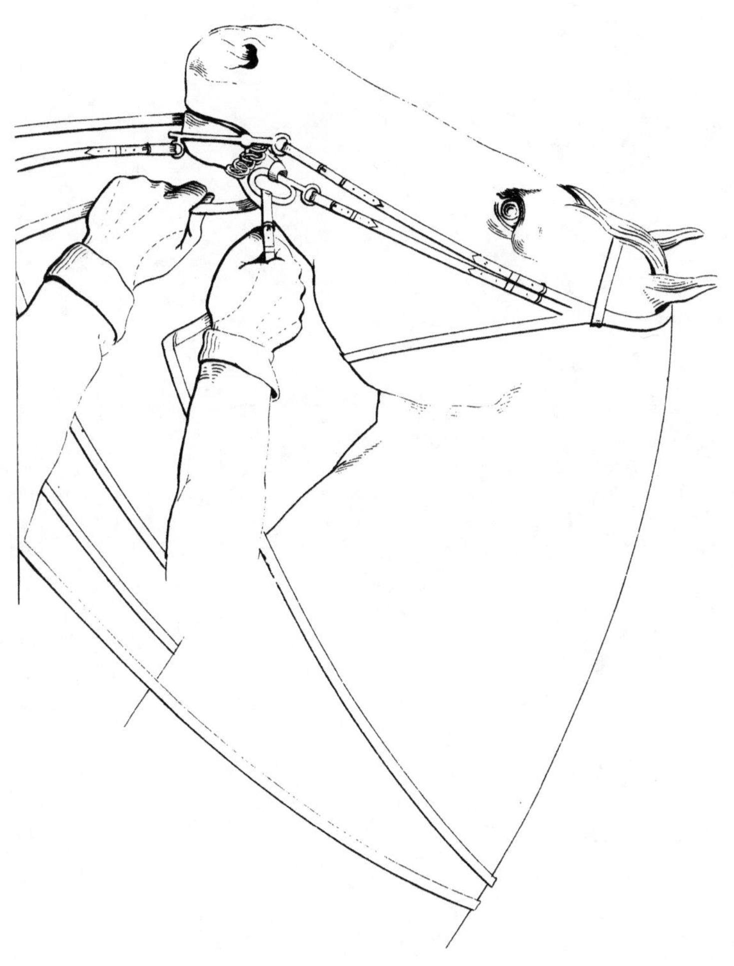

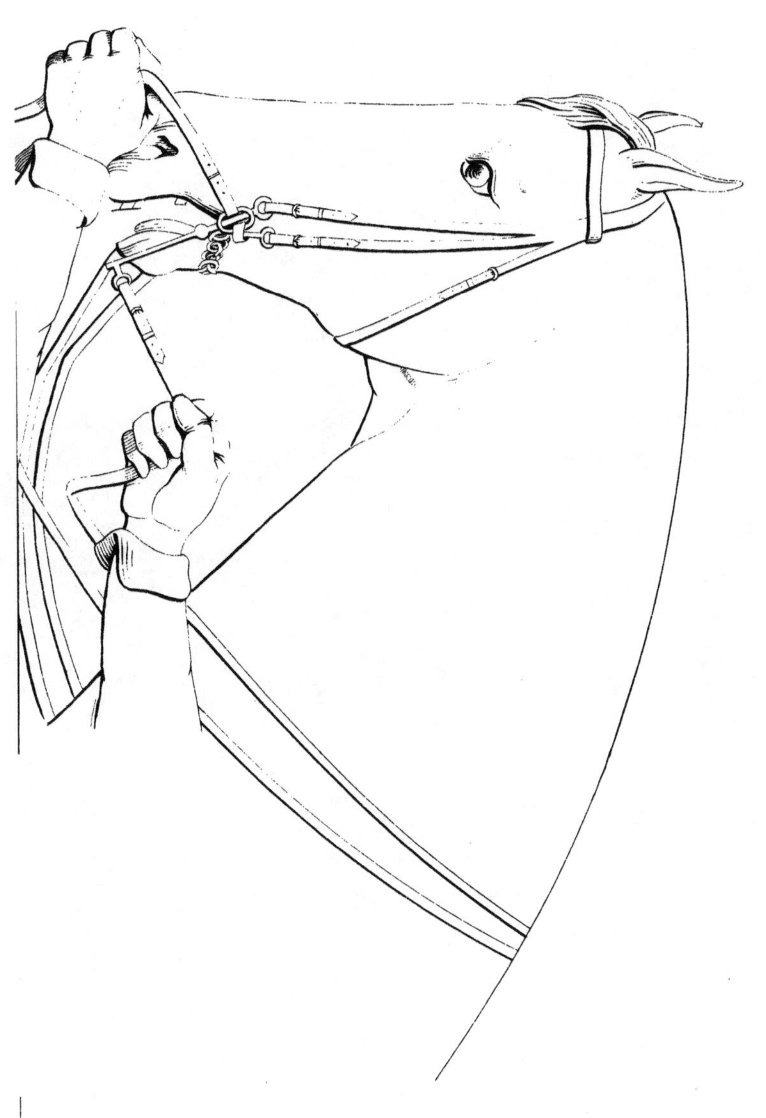

could not have been obtained by any other means. (Plate VI.)

Lateral flexions of the neck.—1. The man will place himself near the horse's shoulder, as for the flexions of the jaw; he will take hold of the right snaffle-rein, which he will draw upon across the neck, in order to establish an intermediate point between the impulsion that comes from him and the resistance the horse presents; he will hold up the left rein with the left hand about a foot from the bit. As soon as the horse endeavors to avoid the constant tension of the right rein by inclining his head to the right, he will let the left rein slip so as to offer no opposition to the flexion of the neck. Whenever the horse endeavors to escape the constraint of the right rein, by bringing his croup around, he will be brought into place again by slight pulls on the left rein. (Plate VII.)

2. When the head and neck have entirely yielded to the right, the man will draw equally on both reins to place the head perpendicularly. Suppleness and lightness will soon follow this position, and as soon as the horse evinces, by champing the bit, entire freedom from stiffness, the man will cease the tension of the reins, being careful that the head does not take advantage of this moment of freedom to displace itself suddenly. In this case, it will be sufficient to restrain it by a slight support of the right rein. After having kept the horse in this position for some seconds, he will make him resume his former position by drawing on the left rein. It is most important that the animal in all his movements should do nothing of his own accord. (Plate VIII.)

The flexion of the neck to the left is executed after the same principles, but by inverse means. The man can repeat with

PL. 7.

PL 8.

Sinclair's Lith

the curb, what he has previously done with the snaffle-reins; but the snaffle should always be employed first, its effect being less powerful and more direct.

When the horse submits without resistance to the preceding exercises, it will prove that the suppling of the neck has already made a great step. The rider can, henceforward, continue his work by operating with a less direct motive power, and without the animal's being impressed by the sight of him. He will place himself in the saddle, and commence by repeating, with the full length of the reins, the lateral flexions, in which he has already exercised his horse.

Lateral flexions of the neck, the man on horseback.—1. To execute the flexion to the right, the rider will take one snaffle-rein in each hand, the left scarcely feeling the bit;

the right, on the contrary, giving a moderate impression at first, but which will increase in proportion to the resistance of the horse, and in a way always to govern him. The animal, soon tired of a struggle which, being prolonged, only makes the pain proceeding from the bit more acute, will understand that the only way to avoid it is to incline the head in the direction from which the pressure is felt. (Plate IX.)

2. As soon as the horse's head is brought round to the right, the left rein will form an opposition, to prevent the nose from passing beyond the perpendicular. Great care should be taken that the head remain always in this position, without which the flexion would be imperfect and the suppleness incomplete. The movement being regularly accomplished, the horse will be made to resume his natural position by a slight tension of the left rein. (Plate X.)

PL. 9.

PL. 10.

The flexion to the left is executed in the same way, the rider employing alternately the snaffle and the curb-reins.

I have already mentioned that it is of great importance to supple the upper part of the neck. After mounting, and having obtained the lateral flexions without resistance, the rider will often content himself with executing them half-way, the head and upper part of the neck pivoting upon the lower part, which will serve as a base, or axis. This exercise must be frequently repeated, even after the horse's education is completed, in order to keep up the pliability of his neck, and facilitate the getting him in hand.

It now remains for us, in order to complete the suppling of the head and neck, to combat the contractions which occasion the direct resistances, and prevent our getting the horse's head into a perpendicular position.

*Direct flexions of the head and neck, or ramener.**—1. The rider will first use the snaffle-reins, which he will hold together in the left hand, as he would the curb-reins. He will rest the outer edge of the right hand (see Plate XI.) upon the reins in front of the left hand, in order to increase the power of the right hand; after which he will gradually bear on the snaffle-bit. As soon as the horse yields, it would suffice to raise the right hand, in order to diminish the tension of the reins, and reward the animal. As the hand must only present a force proportioned to the resistance of the neck, it will only be necessary to hold the legs rather close to prevent backing. When the

* *Ramener* means to place the horse's head in a perpendicular position.—TRANSLATOR.

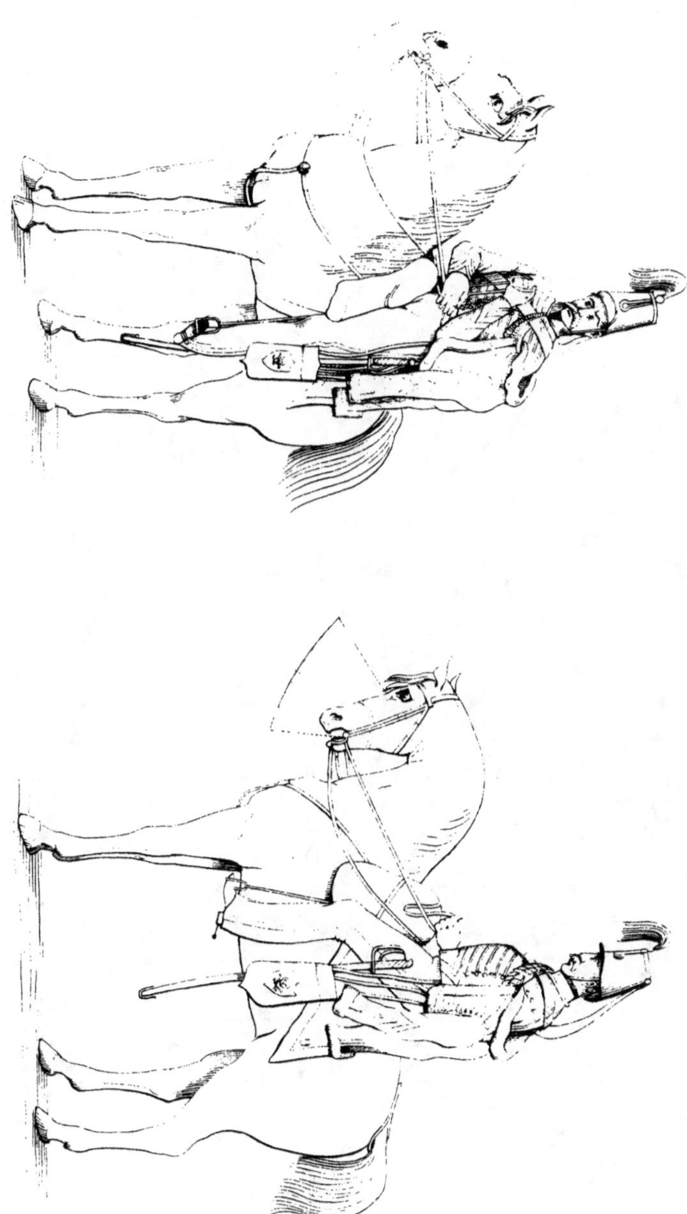

horse obeys the action of the snaffle, he will yield much more quickly to that of the curb, the effect of which is so much more powerful. The curb, of course, needs more care in the use of it than the snaffle. (Plate XI.)

2. The horse will have completely yielded to the action of the hand, when his head is carried in a position perfectly perpendicular to the ground; from that time the contraction will cease, which the animal will show, as in every other case, by champing his bit. The rider must be careful not to be deceived by the feints of the horse, feints which consist in yielding one-fourth or one-third of the way, and then hesitating. If, for example, the nose of the horse having to pass over a curve of ten degrees to attain the perpendicular position (Plate XI.), should stop at the fourth or sixth and again resist, the hand should follow the movement, and then remain firm and immov-

able, for a concession on its part would encourage resistance and increase the difficulties. When the nose shall descend to No. 10, the perpendicular position will be complete, and the lightness perfect. The rider can then cease the tension of the reins, but at the same time he must not permit the head to leave its position. If he lets it return at all to its natural situation, it should only be to draw it back again, and to make the animal understand that the perpendicular position of the head is the only one allowed when under the rider's hand. He should, at the outset, accustom the horse to cease backing at the pressure of the legs, as all backward movements would enable him to avoid the effects of the hand, or create new means of resistance. (Plate XII.)

This is the most important flexion of all; the others tended principally to pave the way for it. As soon as it is executed with ease and promptness, as soon as a slight touch is sufficient to place and keep the head in a perpendicular position, it will prove that the suppling is complete, contraction destroyed, lightness and equilibrium established in the fore-hand. The direction of this part of the animal will, henceforward, be as easy as it is natural, since we have put it in a condition to receive all our impressions, and instantly to yield to them without effort.

As to the functions of the legs, they must support the hind-parts of the horse, in order to obtain the *ramener*, in such a way that he may not be able to avoid the effect of the hand by a retrograde movement of his body. This complete getting in hand is necessary, in order to drive the hind-legs under the centre. In the first case, we act upon the fore-hand; in the second, upon the hind-parts: the first serves for the *ramener*, the second for the *rassembler*, or gathering the horse.*

Combination of effects.—I published four editions of my Method, without devoting a special article to the combination of effects. Although I myself made a very frequent use of it, I had not attached sufficient importance to the great necessity of this principle in the case of teaching; later experiments have taught me to consider it of more consequence.

The combination of effects means the continued and exactly opposed forces of the hand and the legs. Its object should be to bring back again into a position of equili-

* The full meaning of the word *rassembler* will be understood after reading the chapter, further on in this work, under that head. With regard to the word *ramener*, to avoid the constant circumlocution of saying, "placing the horse's head in a perpendicular position," it will be used in future wherever it occurs.—TRANSLATOR.

brium all the parts of the horse which leave it, in order to prevent him from going ahead, without backing him, and *vice versâ:* finally, it serves to stop any movement from the right to the left, or from the left to the right. By this means, also, we distribute the weight of the mass equally on the four legs, and produce temporary immobility. This combination of effects ought to precede and follow each exercise within the graduated limit assigned to it. It is essential when we employ the aids (i. e. the hand and the legs) in this, that the action of the legs should precede that of the hand, in order to prevent the horse from backing against any place; for he might find, in this movement, points of support that would enable him to increase his resistance. Thus, all motion of the extremities, proceeding from the horse himself, should be stopped by a combination of effects; finally, whenever his forces get scattered, and act inharmoniously, the rider will find in this a powerful and infallible corrective.

It is by disposing all the parts of the horse in the most exact order, that we will easily transmit to him the impulsion that should cause the regular movements of his extremities; it is thus also that we will address his comprehension, and that he will appreciate what we demand of him; then will follow caresses of the hand and voice as a moral effect; they should not be used, though, until after he has done what is demanded of him by the rider's hand and legs.

The horse's resting his chin on his breast.— Although few horses are disposed by nature to do this, it is not the less necessary, when it does occur, to practise on them all the flexions, even the one which bends down the neck. In this position, the horse's chin comes back near the breast, and rests in contact with the lower part of the neck; too high a croup, joined to a permanent contraction of the muscles that lower the neck, is generally the cause of it. These muscles must then be suppled in order to destroy their intensity, and thereby give to the muscles that raise the neck, their antagonists, the predominance which will make the neck rest in a graceful and useful position. This first accomplished, the horse will be accustomed to go forward freely at the pressure of the legs, and to respond, without abruptness or excitement, to the touch of the spurs (*attaques*); the object of these last is to bring the hind legs near the centre, and to lower the croup. The rider will then endeavor to raise the horse's head by the aid of the curb-reins; in this case, the hand will be held some distance above the saddle, and far from the body;* the force it transmits to the horse ought to be continued until he yields by elevating his head. As horses of this kind have generally little action, we must take care to avoid letting the hand produce an effect from the front to the rear, in which case it would take away from the impulse necessary for movement. The pace, commencing with the walk, must be kept up at the same rate, while the hand is producing an elevating effect upon the neck. This precept is applicable to all the changes of position that the hand makes in the head and neck; but is particularly essential in the case of a horse disposed to depress his neck.

* This position of the hand at a distance from the saddle and the body will be criticized; but let the rider be reassured; eight or ten lessons will suffice to make the horse change the position of his head, and allow the hand to resume its normal position.

It should be remembered that the horse has two ways of responding to the pressure of the bit; by one he yields, but withdraws himself from it at the same time by shrinking and coming back to his former position. This kind of yielding is only injurious to his education, for if the hand is held too forcibly, if it does not wait till the horse changes of his own accord the position of his head, the backward movement of his body would precede, and be accompanied by a shifting of the weight backwards. In this case, the contraction of his neck remains all the while the same. The second kind of yielding, which contributes so greatly to the rapid and certain education of the horse, is effected by giving a half or three-quarter tension to the reins, sustaining the hand as forcibly as possible without bringing it near the body. In a short time the force of the hand, seconded by the continued pressure of the legs, will make the horse avoid this slight but constant pressure of the bit, but by means of his head and neck only. Then the rider will only make use of the force necessary to displace the head. It is by this means that he will be able to place the horse's body on a level, and will obtain that equilibrium,* the perfect balance

* The word equilibrium, so often repeated in the course of this work, must be categorically explained. People have never rightly understood what is meant by this true equilibrium of a horse, which serves as the basis of his education, and by which he takes instantly, at the rider's will, such a pace, or such a change of direction.

It is not here a question of the equilibrium which prevents the horse from falling down, but of that upon which depends his performance, when it is prompt, graceful, and regular, and by means of which his paces are either measured or extended at will.

Equilibrium of Baucher.

Croup ———————————————— *Head.*

Here the weight and the forces are equally distributed.

of which has not hitherto been appreciated.

Resuming what we have just explained in the case of a horse who rests his chin on his breast, we repeat that it is by producing one force from the rear to the front with the legs, and another from below upwards with the hand, that we will soon be enabled to improve the position and movements of the horse. So that, whatever may be his disposition, it is by first causing the depression of the neck that we will gain a masterly and perfect elevation of it.

I will close this chapter by some reflections on the supposed difference of sensibility in horses' mouths, and the kind of bit which ought to be used.

By means of this just distribution, the different positions, the different paces, and the equilibriums that belong to them, are obtained without effort on the part of man or horse.

Of the horse's mouth and the bit.—I have already treated this subject at length in my Comprehensive Dictionary of Equitation; but as in this work I make a complete exposition of my method, I think it necessary to repeat it in a few words.

I cannot imagine how people have been able so long to attribute to the mere difference of formation of the bars,* those contrary dispositions of horses which render them so light or so hard to the hand. How can we believe that, according as a horse has one or two lines of flesh, more or less, between the bit and the bone of the lower jaw, he should yield to the lightest impulse of the hand, or become unmanageable in spite of all the efforts of two vigorous arms? Nevertheless, it is from remaining in this

* The bars are the continuations, of the two bones of the lower jaw, between the masticating and the front teeth. It is on these that the bit rests.

inconceivable error, that people have forged bits of so strange and various forms, real instruments of torture, the effect of which is to increase the difficulties they sought to remove.

Had they gone back a little further, to the source of the resistances, they would have discovered that this one, like all the rest, does not proceed from the difference of formation of a feeble organ like the bars, but from a contraction communicated to the different parts of the body, and above all to the neck, by some serious fault of constitution. It is then in vain that we attach to the reins, and place in the horse's mouth a more or less murderous instrument; he will remain insensible to our efforts, so long as we do not communicate to him that suppleness which alone can enable him to yield.

In the first place, then, I lay down as a fact, that there is no difference of sensibility in the mouths of horses; that all present the same lightness, when in the position called *ramener*, and the same resistances, in proportion as they recede from this position. There are horses hard to the hand; but this hardness proceeds from the length or weakness of their loins, from a narrow croup, from short haunches, thin thighs, straight hocks, or (a most important point) from a croup too high or too low in proportion to the withers: such are the true causes of resistances. The contraction of the neck, the closing of the jaws, are only the effects; and as to the bars, they are only there to show the ignorance of self-styled equestrian theoricians. By suppling the neck and the jaw, this hardness completely disappears. Experiments, a hundred times repeated, give me the right to advance this principle boldly; perhaps it may, at first, appear too arbitrary, but it is none the less true.

Consequently, I only allow one kind of bit, and this is the form and the dimensions I give it, to make it as simple as it is easy.

The branches straight and six inches long, measuring from the eye of the bit to the extremity of the branch; circumference of the canon* two inches and a half; port, about two inches wide at the bottom, and one inch at the top. The only variation to be in the width of the bit, according to the horse's mouth.

I insist that such a bit is sufficient to render passively obedient all horses that have been prepared by supplings; and I need not add that, as I deny the utility of severe bits, I reject all means not coming directly from the rider, such as martingales, piliers, &c.

* The mouth-piece of the bit consists of three parts: the port, to give freedom to the tongue, and the two canons, which are the parts that come in contact with the bars.—TRANSLATOR.

IV.

CONTINUATION OF SUPPLINGS.

The hind-parts.—In order to guide the horse, the rider acts directly on two of his parts; the fore-parts and the hind-parts. To effect this he employs two motive powers: the legs, which give the impulse by the croup; and the hand, which directs and modifies this impulse by the head and neck. A perfect harmony of forces ought then to exist always between these two motive powers; but the same harmony is equally necessary between the parts of the animal which they are intended particularly to impress. Our labor to render the head and neck flexible, light, and obedient to the touch of the hand, would be vain, its results incomplete, and the equilibrium of the whole animal imperfect, so long as the croup remained dull, contracted, and rebellious to the direct governing agent.

I have just explained the simple and easy means of giving to the fore parts the qualities indispensable to their good management; it remains to tell how we will fashion, in the same way, the hind parts, in order to complete the suppling of the horse, and bring about a uniform harmony in the development of all his moving parts. The resistances of the neck and croup mutually aiding one another, our labor will be more easy, as we have already destroyed the opposition of the former.

The flexions of the croup, and making it movable.—1. The rider will hold the curb-reins in the left hand, and those of the snaffle, crossed, in the right, the nails of the right hand held downward; he will first bring the horse's head into a perpendicular position, by drawing lightly on the bit; after that, if he wishes to execute the movement to the right, he will carry the left leg back behind the girths and fix it near the flanks of the animal, until the croup yields to this pressure. The rider will at the same time make the left snaffle-rein felt, proportioning the effect of the rein to the resistance which is opposed to it. Of these two forces, thus transmitted by the left leg and the rein of the same side, the first is intended to combat the resistance, and the second, to determine the movement. The rider should content himself in the beginning with making the croup execute one or two steps only sideways. (Plate XIII.)

2. The croup having acquired more facility in moving, we can continue the movement so as to complete reversed pirouettes to the right and the left.* As soon as the

* See note, page 117.

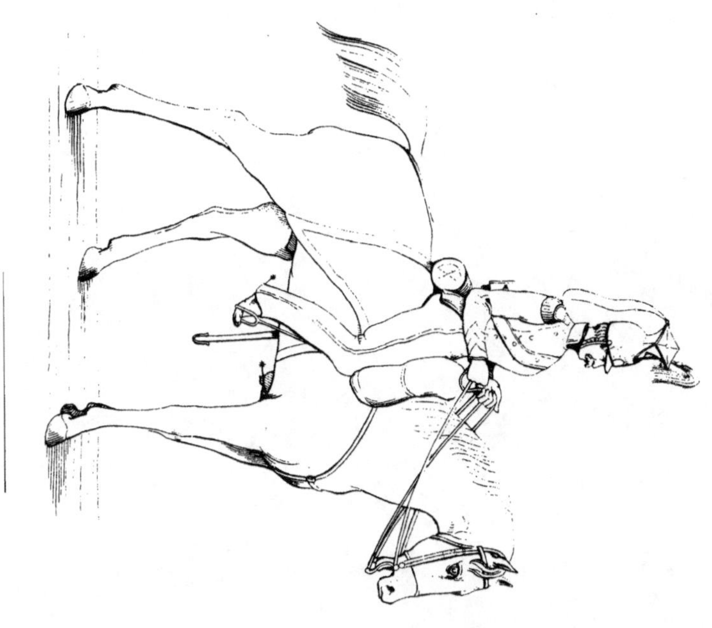

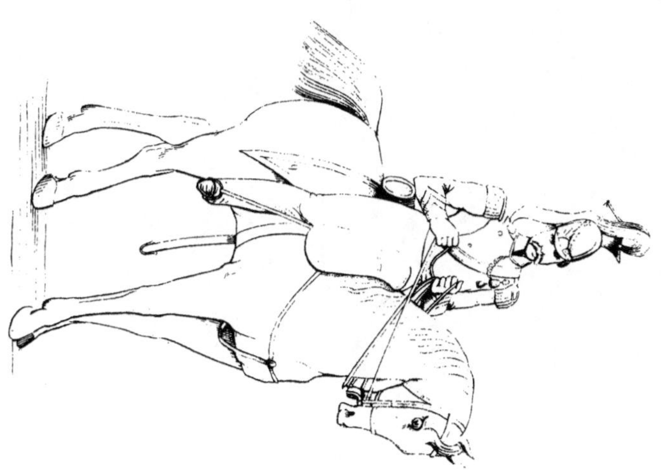

haunches yield to the pressure of the leg, the rider, to cause the perfect equilibrium of the horse, will immediately draw upon the rein opposite to this leg. The motion of this, slight at first, will be progressively increased until the head is inclined to the side towards which the croup is moving, as if to look at it coming. (Plate XIV.)

To make this movement understood, I will add some explanations, the more important as they are applicable to all the exercises of horsemanship.

The horse, in all his movements, cannot preserve a perfect and constant equilibrium, without a combination of opposite forces, skilfully managed by the rider. In the reversed pirouette, for example, if when the horse has yielded to the pressure of the leg, we continue to oppose the rein on the same side as this leg, it is evident that we will shoot beyond the mark, since we will be employing a force which has become useless. We must then establish two motive powers, the effect of which balances, without interfering; this, the tension of the rein on the opposite side from the leg will produce in the pirouette. So, we will commence with the rein and the leg of the same side; when it is time to pass to the second part of the work, we will employ the curb-rein in the left hand, and finally, the snaffle-rein opposite to the leg. The forces will then be kept in a diagonal position, and in consequence, the equilibrium natural, and the execution of the movement easy. The horse's head being turned to the side where the croup is moving, adds much to the gracefulness of the performance, and aids the rider in regulating the activity of the haunches, and keeping the shoulders in place. For the rest, tact alone will be able to show him how to use the leg and the rein, in such a way that their motions will mutually sustain, without at any time counteracting one another.

I need not remind you that during the whole of this exercise, as on all occasions, the neck should remain supple and light; the head in position (perpendicular) and the jaw movable. While the bridle hand keeps them in this proper position, the right hand, with the aid of the snaffle, is combating the lateral resistances, and determining the different inclinations, until the horse is sufficiently well broken to obey a simple pressure of the bit. If, when combating the contraction of the croup, we permitted the horse to throw its stiffness into the fore parts, our efforts would be vain, and the fruit of our first labors lost. On the contrary, we will facilitate the subjection of the hind parts, by preserving the advantages we have already acquired over the fore parts, and by keeping separated those contractions we have yet to combat.

The leg of the rider opposite to that which determines the rotation of the croup, must not be kept off during the movement, but remain close to the horse and keep him in place, while giving from the rear forward an impulse which the other leg communicates from right to left, or from left to right. There will thus be one force which keeps the horse in position, and another which determines the rotation. In order that the pressure of the two legs should not counteract one another, and in order to be able to use them both together, the leg intended to move the croup will be placed farther behind the girths than the other, which will remain held with a force equal to that of the leg which determines the movement. Then the action of the legs will be distinct, the one bearing from right to left, the other from the rear forwards. It is by the aid of the latter that the hand places and fixes the fore legs.

To accelerate these results, at first, a second person may be employed, who will place himself at the height of the horse's head, holding the curb-reins in the right hand, and on the side opposite to which we wish the croup to go. He will lay hold of the reins at six inches from the branches of the bit, so as to be in a good position to combat the instinctive resistances of the animal. The one in the saddle will content himself with holding lightly the snaffle-reins, acting with his legs as I have already shown. The second person is only useful when we have to deal with a horse of an intractable disposition, or to aid the inexperience of the man in the saddle; but, as much should be done without assistance as possible, in order that the practitioner may judge by himself of the progress of his horse, seeking all the while for means to increase the effects of his touch.

Even while this work is in an elementary state, he will make the horse execute easily all the figures of the *manège de deux pistes.** After eight days of moderate exercise, he will have accomplished, without effort, a performance that the old school did not dare to undertake until after two or three years of study and work with the horse.

When the rider has accustomed the croup of the horse to yield promptly to the pressure of the legs, he will be able to put it in motion, or fix it motionless at will, and he

* "*La piste* is an imaginary line upon which the horse is made to walk. When the hind legs follow the same line as the fore ones, the horse is said to go *d'une piste*, or on one line. He goes *de deux pistes*, or on two lines, when his hind legs pass along a line parallel to that traced by the fore legs."—*Baucher's Dictionnaire d'Equitation.*

can, consequently, execute ordinary pirouettes.* For this purpose he will take a snaffle-rein in each hand, one to direct the neck and shoulders towards the side to which we wish to wheel, the other to second the opposite leg, if it be not sufficient to keep the croup still. At the beginning, this leg should be placed as far back as possible, and not be used until the haunches bear against it. By careful and progressive management the results will soon be attained. At the start, the horse should be allowed to

* "The *pirouette* is executed on the fore or hind legs, by making the horse turn round upon himself, in such a way, that the leg on the side he is going, acts as a pivot, and is the principal support around which the other three legs move."—*Baucher's Dictionnaire d'Equitation.*

Pirouettes are either *ordinary* or *reversed.* In the ordinary *pirouette,* one of the hind legs is the pivot on which the horse moves; in the reversed, one of the fore legs.—TRANSLATOR.

rest after executing two or three steps well, which will give five or six halts in the complete rotation of the shoulders around the croup.

Here the stationary exercises cease. I will now explain how the suppling of the hind parts will be completed, by commencing to combine the play of its springs with those of the fore parts.

Backing.—The retrograde movement, otherwise called backing, is an exercise, the importance of which has not been sufficiently appreciated, and which yet ought to have a very great influence upon his education. When practised after the old erroneous methods, it was of no use, as the exercises that should precede it were unknown. Backing properly differs essentially from that incorrect backward movement, which carries the horse to the rear with his croup contracted and his neck stiff; that is backing away from and avoiding the effect of the reins. Backing correctly supples the horse, and adds grace and precision to his natural motions. The first of the conditions upon which it is to be obtained, is to keep the horse in hand, that is to say, supple, light in the mouth, steady on his legs, and perfectly balanced in all his parts. Thus disposed, the animal will be able with ease to move and elevate equally his fore and hind legs.

It is here that we will be enabled to appreciate the good effects and the indispensable necessity of suppling the neck and haunches. Backing, which at first is tolerably painful to the horse, will always lead him to combat the motions of our hand, by stiffening his neck, and those of our legs, by contracting his croup; these are the instinctive resistances. If we cannot obviate the bad disposition of them, how will we be able to obtain that shifting and reshifting of weight, which alone can make the execution of this movement perfect? If the impulsion which, in backing, ought to come from the fore parts, should pass over its proper limits, the movement would become painful, impossible in fact, and occasion on the part of the animal, sudden, violent movements which are always injurious to his organization.

On the other hand, the displacements* of the croup, by destroying the harmony which should exist between the relative forces of fore and hind parts, would also hinder the proper execution of the backing. The previous exercise to which we have subjected the croup will aid us in keeping it in a

* These displacements of the croup mean sideway displacement, or the horse's croup not being in a line with the shoulders.—TRANSLATOR.

straight line with the shoulders, in order to preserve the necessary transferring of the forces and weight.

To commence the movement, the rider ought first to assure himself that the haunches are on a line with the shoulders, and the horse light in hand; then he will slowly close his legs, in order that the action which they will communicate to the hind parts of the horse may make him lift one of his hind legs, and prevent the body from yielding before the neck. It is then that the immediate pressure of the bit, forcing the horse to regain his equilibrium behind, will produce the first part of the backing. As soon as the horse obeys, the rider will instantly give the hand to reward the animal, and not to force the play of his fore parts. If his croup be displaced, the rider will bring it back by means of his leg, and if necessary, use for this purpose the snaffle-rein on that side.

After having defined what I call the proper backing (*reculer*), I ought to explain what I understand by backing so as to avoid the bit (*l'acculement*). This movement is too painful to the horse, too ungraceful, and too much opposed to the right development of his mechanism, not to have struck any one who has occupied himself at all with horsemanship. We force a horse backwards in this way, whenever we crowd his forces and weight too much upon his hind parts; by so doing we destroy his equilibrium, and render grace, measure, and correctness impossible. Lightness, always lightness! this is the basis, the touchstone of all beautiful execution. With this, all is easy, for the horse as well as the rider. That being the case, it is understood that the difficulty of horsemanship does not consist in the direction to give the horse, but in the position to make him assume—a position which alone can smooth all obstacles. Indeed, if the horse executes, it is the rider who makes him do so; upon him then rests the responsibility of every false movement.

It will suffice to exercise the horse for eight days (for five minutes each lesson) in backing, to make him execute it with facility. The rider will content himself the first few times with one or two steps to the rear, followed by the combined effect of the legs and hand, increasing in proportion to the progress he makes, until he finds no more difficulty in a backward than in a forward movement.

What an immense step we will then have made in the education of our pupil! At the start, the defective formation of the animal, his natural contractions, the resistances we encountered everywhere, seemed as if they might defy our efforts, for ever.

Without doubt they would have been vain, had we made use of a bad course of proceeding; but the wise system of progression that we have introduced into our work, the destruction of the instinctive forces of the horse, the suppling, the separate subjection of all the rebellious parts, have soon placed in our power the whole of his mechanism to a degree which enables us to govern it completely, and to restore that pliability, ease, and harmony of the parts, which their bad arrangement threatened always to prevent. As I shall point out hereafter, in classing the general division of the labor, it will be seen that eight or ten days are sufficient to obtain these important results.

Was I not right then in saying that if it is not in my power to change the defective formation of a horse, I can yet prevent the consequences of his physical defects, so as to render him as fit to do everything with grace and natural ease, as the better-formed horse? In suppling the parts of the animal upon which the rider acts directly, in order to govern and guide him, in accustoming them to yield without difficulty or hesitation to the different impressions which are communicated to them, I have destroyed their stiffness, and restored the centre of gravity to its true place, namely, to the middle of the body. I have, besides, settled the greatest difficulty of horsemanship: that of subjecting, before everything else, the parts upon which the rider acts directly, in order to prepare for him infallible means of impressing his will upon the horse.

It is only by destroying the instinctive forces, and by suppling the different parts of the horse, that we can obtain this. All the springs of the animal's body are thus yielded up to the discretion of the rider. But this first advantage will not be enough to make him a complete horseman. The employment of these forces thus abandoned to him, demand, in order to execute the different paces, much study and skill. I will show in the subsequent chapters the rules to be observed. I will conclude this one by a rapid recapitulation of the progression to be followed in the supplings.

Stationary exercise, the rider on foot. Fore-parts.—1. Flexions of the jaw to the right and left, using the curb-bit.

2. Direct flexions of the jaw, and depression of the neck.

3. Lateral flexions of the neck with the snaffle-reins and with the curb.

Stationary exercise, the rider on horseback.—1. Lateral flexions of the neck with the snaffle-reins, and with the curb-reins.

2. Direct flexions of the head, or placing

it in a perpendicular position with the snaffle, and with the curb-reins.

Hind-parts.—3. Lateral flexions, and moving the croup around the shoulders.

4. Rotation of the shoulders around the haunches.

5. Combining the play of the fore and hind legs of the horse, or backing.

I have placed the rotation of the shoulders around the haunches in the nomenclature of stationary exercise. But the ordinary pivoting, or *pirouette*, being a pretty complicated movement, and a difficult one for the horse, he should not be completely exercised in it until he has acquired the measured time of the walk, and of the trot, and can easily execute the changes of direction.

V.

OF THE EMPLOYMENT OF THE FORCES OF THE HORSE BY THE RIDER.

When the supplings have subjected the instinctive forces of the horse, and given them up completely into our power, the animal will be nothing more in our hands than a passive, expectant machine, ready to act upon any impulsion we choose to communicate to him. It will be for us, then, as sovereign disposers of all his forces, to combine the employment of them in correct proportion to the movements we wish to execute.

The young horse, at first stiff and awkward in the use of his members, will need a certain degree of management in developing them. In this, as in every other case, we will follow that rational progression which tells us to commence with the simple, before passing to the complicated. By the preceding exercise, we have made our means of acting upon the horse sure. We must now attend to facilitating his means of execution, by exercising all his forces together. If the animal respond to the aids of the rider by the jaw, the neck, and the haunches; if he yield, by the general disposition of his body, to the impulses communicated to him, it is by the play of his extremities that he executes the movement. The mechanism of these parts ought then to be easy, prompt, and regular; their application, well directed in the different paces, can alone give them such qualities as are indispensable to a good education.*

* It must not be forgotten that the hand and legs have their vocabulary also; and a very concise one.

The walk.—This pace is the mother of all the other paces; by it we will obtain the cadence, the regularity, and the extension of the others. But to obtain these brilliant results, the rider must display as much knowledge as tact. The preceding exercises have led the horse to bear the combined effect of hand and legs, which could not have been done previously to the destruction of his instinctive resistances; we have now only to act on the inert resistances which appertain to the animal's weight; upon the forces which move only when an impulse is communicated to them.

Before making the horse go forward, we

This mute, laconic language consists of these few words. *You are doing badly; this is what you should do; you do well now.* It is sufficient for the rider to be able to translate, by his mechanism, the meaning of these three remarks, to possess all the equestrian erudition, and share his intelligence with his horse.

should first assure ourselves of his lightness, that is to say of his head being perpendicular, his neck flexible, his hind parts straight and plumb. The legs will then be closed lightly, to give the body the impulse necessary to move it. But we should not, in accordance with the precepts of the old method, give the bridle hand at the same time; for then the neck, being free from all restraint, would lose its lightness, would contract, and render the motion of the hand powerless. The rider will remember that his hand ought to be to the horse an insurmountable barrier, whenever he would leave the position of *ramener*. Then the animal will never attempt it, without pain; and only within our limit will he find ease and comfort. By the application of my method, the rider will be led to guide his horse at all times with the reins half tight, except when he wishes to correct a false movement, or determine a new one.

The walk, I have said, ought to precede the other paces, because the horse having three supports upon the ground, his action is less, and consequently easier to regulate than in the trot and the gallop. The first exercises of the supplings will be followed by some turns in the riding-house at a walk, but only as a relaxation, the rider attending less to animating his horse, than to making him keep his head, while walking, in a perpendicular position. Little by little he will complicate his work, so as to join to the lightness of the horse that precision of movement indispensable to the beauty of all his paces.

He will commence light oppositions of the hand and legs, to make the forces of the fore and hind parts work together in harmony. This exercise, by accustoming the horse always to yield the use of his forces to the direction of the rider, will be also useful in forming his intelligence, as well as in developing his powers. What delights the expert horseman will experience in the progressive application of his art! His pupil, at first rebellious, will insensibly yield himself to his every wish; will adopt his character, and end by becoming the living personification of him. Take care, then, rider! If your horse is capricious, violent, fantastic, we will have the right to say that you yourself do not shine by the amenity of your disposition, and the propriety of your proceedings.

In order to keep the measure and quickness of the walk equal and regular, it is indispensable that the impulsive and governing forces which come from the rider, should themselves be in perfect harmony. We will suppose, for example, that the rider to move his horse forward, should make use of a force equal to twenty pounds, fifteen for the impulse forward, and five to bring his head into position. If the legs increase their motion without the hands increasing theirs in the same proportion, it is evident that the surplus of communicated force will be thrown into the neck, cause it to contract, and destroy all lightness. If, on the contrary, it is the hand which acts with too much violence, it will be at the expense of the impulsive force necessary to move the horse forward; on this account, his forward movement will be slackened and counteracted, at the same time that his position will lose its gracefulness and power.

This short explanation will suffice to show the harmony that should exist between the legs and hands. It is understood that their motion should vary according as the formation of the horse renders it necessary to support him more or less before or behind; but the rule is the same, only the proportions are different.

So long as the horse will not keep himself supple and light in his walk, we will continue to exercise him in a straight line; but as soon as he acquires more ease and steadiness, we will commence to make him execute changes of direction to the right and the left, while walking.

Changes of direction.—The use of the wrists, in the changes of direction, is so simple that it is unnecessary to speak of it here. I will only call attention to the fact, that the resistances of the horse ought always to be anticipated by disposing his forces in such a manner that they all concur in putting him in the way of moving. The head will be inclined in the direction we wish to go by means of the snaffle-rein of that side, the curb will then complete the movement. General rule: the lateral resistances of the neck are always to be opposed by the aid of the snaffle, being very careful not to commence to wheel until after destroying the obstacle that opposed it. If the use of the wrists remains very nearly the same as formerly, it is not so with the legs; their motion will be diametrically opposite to that given them in the old style of horsemanship. This innovation is so natural a one, that I cannot conceive why some one did not apply it before me.

It is by bearing the hand to the right and making the right leg felt, people have told me, (and I myself at first repeated it,) that the horse is made to turn to the right. With me, practice has always taken the precedence of reasoning; and this is the way I first perceived the incorrectness of this principle.

Whatever lightness my horse had in a

straight line, I remarked that this lightness always lost some of its delicacy when moving in small circles, although my outside leg came to the assistance of the inside one. As soon as the hind leg put itself in motion to follow the shoulders in the circle, I immediately felt a slight resistance. I then thought of changing the use of my aids, and of pressing the leg on the side opposite to the direction of wheeling. At the same time, in place of bearing the hand immediately to the right, to determine the shoulders in that direction, I first, by the aid of this hand, made the opposition necessary to render the haunches motionless, and to dispose the forces in such a way as to maintain the equilibrium during the execution of the movement. This proceeding was completely successful; and in explaining what ought to be the functions of the different extremities, I recognize this as the only rational way of using them in wheeling.

In fact, in wheeling to the right, for example, it is the right hind leg which serves as pivot and supports the whole weight of the mass, while the left hind leg and the fore legs describe a circle more or less extended. In order that the movement should be correct and free, it is necessary that this pivot, upon which the whole turns, be not interfered with in its action; the simultaneous use of the right hand and the right leg must necessarily produce this effect. The equilibrium is thus destroyed, and the regularity of the wheeling rendered impossible.

As soon as the horse executes easily the changes of direction at a walk, and keeps himself perfectly light, we can commence exercising at a trot.

The trot.—The rider will commence this

pace at a very moderate rate of speed, following exactly the same principles as for the walk. He will keep his horse perfectly light, not forgetting that the faster the pace, the more disposition there will be, on the part of the animal, to fall back again into his natural contractions. The hand should then be used with redoubled nicety, in order to keep the head and neck always pliable, without effecting the impulse necessary to the movement. The legs will lightly second the hands, and the horse between these two barriers, which are obstacles only to his improper movements, will soon develop all his best faculties; and with precision of movement, he will also acquire grace, extension, and the steadiness inherent to the lightness of the whole.

Although many persons who would not take the trouble to examine thoroughly my method, have pretended that it is opposed to great speed in trotting, it is not the less proved that the well-balanced horse can trot faster than the one destitute of this advantage. I have given proofs of this whenever they have been demanded of me; but it is in vain that I have tried to make people understand what constitutes the motions of the trot, and what are the conditions indispensable for regularity in executing it. So, I was obliged in a race, of which I was judge, to make the bets void, and to prove that the pretended trotters were really not trotting, but ambling.

The condition indispensable to a good trotter is perfect equilibrium of the body. Equilibrium, which keeps up a regular movement of the diagonal fore and hind feet, gives them an equal elevation and extension, with such lightness that the animal can easily execute all changes of direction, moderate his speed, halt, or increase his speed without effort. The fore parts have not, then, the appearance of towing after them the hind parts, which keep as far off as possible; everything becomes easy and graceful for the horse, because his forces, being in perfect harmony, permit the rider to dispose of them in such a way that they mutually and constantly assist each other.

It would be impossible for me to count up the number of horses that have been sent to me to break, whose paces have been so spoiled that it was impossible for them to trot a single step. A few lessons have always been sufficient to get them back into regular paces, and these are the means I employed.

The difficulty which the horse experiences in keeping himself square in his trot, almost always proceeds from the hind parts. Whether these be of a feeble construction, or be rendered useless by the superior vigor of the fore parts, the motions of these parts, which receive the shock and give the bound, in each case become powerless, and in consequence render the movement irregular.* There is, then,

* I am not of the opinion of those connoisseurs who imagine that the qualities of the horse, as well as his speed in trotting, depend principally on the height of his withers. I think that, for the horse to be stylish and regular in his movements, the croup should be on a level with the withers; such was the construction of the old English horses. A certain kind of horses, very much *à la mode*, called steppers, are constructed after an entirely different fashion; they strike out with their fore legs, and drag their hind parts after them. Horses with a low croup, or with withers very high in proportion to their croup, were preferred by horsemen of the old school, and are still in favor nowadays among amateur horsemen. The German horsemen have an equally marked predilection for this sort of formation, although it is contrary to strength of the croup, to the equilibrium of the horse, and to the regular play of his feet and legs. This fault

weakness in one extremity, or excess of force in the other. The remedy in each case will be the same, viz.: the depression of the neck, which, by diminishing the power of the fore parts, restores the equilibrium between the two parts. We have practised this suppling on foot; it will be easy to obtain it on horseback. We here see the usefulness of this perpendicular flexion, which allows us to place on a level

of construction (for it is one) has been scarcely noticed till now; nevertheless, it is a great one, and really retards the horse's education. In fact, we are obliged, in order to render his movements uniform, to lower his neck, so that the kind of lever it represents may serve to lighten his hind parts of the weight with which they are overburdened. I ought also to say, that this change of position, or of equilibrium, is only obtained by the aid of my principles. I explain the cause and effect, and I point out the remedies. Is this not the proper way for an author to proceed?

the forces of the two opposite extremities of the horse, in order to make them harmonious, and induce regularity in their working. The horse being thus placed, can bend and extend his fore and hind legs, before the weight of the body forces them to resume their support.

The practice of this and some other principles that I explain in this work, will place in the rank of choice horses animals whose inferiority caused them to be considered jades, and which the old method would never have raised from their degradation. It will suffice, to accustom the horse to trot well, to exercise him at this pace only five minutes in each lesson. When he acquires the necessary ease and lightness, he can be made to execute ordinary *pirouettes,* as well as the exercise on two lines, at a walk and a trot. I have said that five minutes of trotting were enough at first, because it is less the continuance of an exercise than its being properly done that perfects the execution of it. Besides, as this pace requires a considerable displacement of forces, and as the animal will have been already subjected to a rather painful exercise, it would be dangerous to prolong it beyond the time I mentioned. The horse will lend himself more willingly to your efforts when they are nicely managed, and of short duration; his intelligence, becoming familiar with this efficient progression, will hasten success. He will submit himself calmly, and without repugnance, to work in which there will be nothing painful to him; and we will be able thus to push his education to the farthest limits, not only without injury to his physical organization, but in restoring to their normal state organs which a forced exercise might have weakened. This regular development of all the organs of the horse will not only give him grace, but also strength and health: thus prolonging his existence, while increasing a hundredfold the delights of the true horseman.

VI.

OF THE CONCENTRATION OF THE FORCES OF THE HORSE BY THE RIDER.

THE rider now understands that the only means of obtaining precision and regularity of movement in the walk and the trot, is to keep the horse perfectly light while he is exercised at these paces. As soon as we are sure of this lightness, while going in a straight line, in changes of direction, and in circular movements, it will be easy to preserve it while exercising on two lines.

I would here treat immediately of the gallop; but this pace, more complicated than the other two, demands an arrangement on the part of the horse, and a power on the part of the rider, that the preceding exercises have not yet given. The proper placing of the horse's head spreads his forces over the whole of his body; it is necessary, in order to perform correctly the different exercises at a gallop, and to enable yourself properly to direct the forces in energetic movements, to bring them into a common focus—that is, to the centre of gravity of the animal. I am about to explain how this is to be done.

The use of the spurs.—Professors of equitation and authors upon this subject have said, that the spurs are to punish the horse when he does not respond to the legs, or when he refuses to approach an object that frightens him. With them, the spur is not an aid, but a means of chastisement. With me it is, on the contrary, a powerful auxiliary, without which it would be impossible to break any horse perfectly. How! you exclaim; you attack with the spur horses that are sensitive, excitable, full of fire and action—horses whose powerful make leads them to become unmanageable, in spite of the hardest bits and the most vigorous arms! Yes, and it is with the spur that I will moderate the fury of these too fiery animals, and stop them short in their most impetuous bounds. It is with the spur, aided of course by the hand, that I will make the most stubborn natures kind, and perfectly educate the most intractable animal.

Long before publishing my "*Comprehensive Dictionary of Equitation*," I was aware of the excellent effects of the spur; but I abstained from developing my principles, being prevented by an expression of one of my friends, whom I had shown how to obtain results which to him appeared miraculous. "It is extraordinary! It is wonderful!" he exclaimed; "but it is a razor in the hands of a monkey." It is true that the use of the spurs requires prudence, tact, and gradation; but the effects of it are precious. Now that I have proved the efficacy of my method; now that I see my most violent adversaries become warm partisans of my principles, I no longer fear to develop a process that I consider one of the most beautiful results of my long researches in horsemanship.

There is no more difference in the sensibility of different horses' flanks than in their sensibility of mouth—that is to say, the direct effect of the spur is nearly the same in them all. I have already shown that the organization of the bars of the mouth goes for nothing in its resistances to the hand. It is clear enough that if the nose, by being thrown up in the air, gives the horse a force of resistance equal to two hundred pounds, this force will be reduced to one hundred pounds, when we bring the horse's head half way towards a perpendicular position; to fifty pounds when brought still nearer that position, and to nothing when perfectly placed. The pretended hardness of mouth proceeds, in this case, from a bad position of the head, which is caused by the stiffness of the neck and the faulty construction of the loins and haunches of the horse. If we carefully examine the causes that produce what is called sensibility of the flanks, we will discover that they have very much the same kind of source.

The innumerable conjectures to which people have devoted themselves, in attributing to the horse's flanks a local sensibility that had no existence, have necessarily injured the progress of his education, because it was based upon false data. The greater or less sensibility of the animal proceeds from his action, from his faulty formation, and the bad position resulting therefrom. To a horse of natural action, but with long, weak loins, and bad action behind, every motion backwards is painful; and the very disposition that leads him to rush ahead, serves him to avoid the pain of the spur. He returns to this movement whenever he feels the rider's legs touch him; and far from being a spirited horse, he is only scared and crazy. The more he fears the spur, the more he plunges out of hand, and baffles the means intended to make him obedient. There is everything to fear from such a horse; he will scare at objects from the very ease he possesses of avoiding them. Now since his fright proceeds, so to say, from the bad position we allow him to take, this inconvenience will disappear from the moment we remedy the first cause of it. We must confine the forces in order to prevent every displacement. We must separate the *physical* from the *moral* horse, and force these impressions to concentrate in the brain. He will then be a furious madman, whose limbs we have bound to prevent him from carrying his frenzied thoughts into execution.

The best proof we have that the promptness of a horse in responding to the effect of the legs and spurs, is not caused by a sensibility of the flanks, but rather by great action joined to bad formation, is that the same action is not so manifest in a well-formed horse, and that the latter bears the spur much better than one whose equilibrium and organization are inferior.

But the spur is not only useful in moderating the too great energy of horses of much action; its effect being equally good in combating that disposition which leads the animal to throw his centre of gravity too much forward, or back. I would also use it to stir up those that are wanting in ardor and vivacity. In horses of action, the forces of the hind parts surpass those of the fore parts. It is the opposite in dull horses. We can thus account for the quickness of the former; the slowness and sluggishness of the latter.

By the exercise of suppling, we have completely annulled the instinctive forces of the horse. We must now reunite these forces in their true centre of gravity, which is the middle of the animal's body; and it is by the properly combined opposition of the legs and hands that we will succeed in this. The advantages we possess already over the horse, will enable us to combat, from their very birth, all the resistances which tend to make him leave the proper position—the only one in which we can successfully practise our oppositions. It is also of the first importance to put into our proceedings tact and gradation, so that, for example, the legs never give an impulse that the hand is not able to take hold of and govern at the same moment. I will make this principle more clear by a short explanation.

We will suppose a horse at a walk, employing a force of forty pounds, which is necessary to keep the pace regular, till the moment when the opposition of the hand and legs commences. By and by we begin a slow and gradual pressure of the legs, which adds ten pounds to the impulse of the pace. As the horse is supposed to be perfectly in hand, the hand will immediately feel this passage of forces, and must then make itself master of them to transfer them to the centre. Meanwhile the legs will continue their pressure, to the end that the forces, thus driven back, may not return to the focus which they left; for that would be but a useless ebbing and flowing of förces. This succession of oppositions, well combined, will bring together a great quantity of forces in the centre of the horse's body, and the more these are increased, the more the animal will lose his instinctive energy. When the pressure of the legs becomes insufficient to collect the forces entirely, more energetic means must be employed, viz.: touches of the spur.

The spurring ought not to be done violently, and with much movement of the legs, but with delicacy and management. The rider ought to close his legs so gradually that, before coming in actual contact with the horse's flanks, the spur will not be more than a hair's breadth from them, if possible. The hand should ever be an echo to the light touches with which we commence; and it should be firmly held, so as to present an opposition equal to the force communicated by the spur. If by the time being badly chosen, the hand does not exactly intercept the impulse given, and a general commotion results therefrom, we should, before recommencing, gather the horse together, and re-establish calm in his motions. The force of the spurring will be progressively increased until the horse bears it, when as vigorously applied as possible, without presenting the least resistance to the hand, without increasing the speed of his pace, or without displacing himself so long as we operate with a firm foot.

A horse brought thus to bear spurring, is three-fourths broken, since we have the free disposition of all his forces. Besides, his centre of gravity being where his forces are all united, we have brought it to its proper place, viz.: the middle of the body. All the oscillations of the animal will then be subordinate to us, and we will be able to

14

transfer his weight with ease, when necessary.

It is easy now to understand where the resistances have their origin; whether the horse kicks up behind, rears, or runs away, the cause is always the centre of gravity being in the wrong place. This very cause belongs to a defective formation which we cannot change, it is true, but the effects of which we can always modify. If the horse kicks up, the centre of gravity is in the shoulders, in the croup when he rears, and too far forward when he runs away. The principal thought of the rider, then, ought to be to keep the centre of gravity in the middle of the horse's body, since he will thereby prevent him defending himself, and bring back the forces of the badly formed horse to the place which they occupy in the finest organizations. It is this that makes me assert that a well-formed horse will not make resistance nor move irregularly, for it requires supernatural efforts on his part to destroy the harmony of his moving parts, and so greatly displace his centre of gravity. So, when I speak of the necessity of giving the horse a new equilibrium, in order to prevent his defending himself, and also to remedy the ungracefulness of his form, I allude to the combination of forces of which I have been treating, or, rather, of the removal of the centre of gravity from one place to another. This result obtained, the education of the horse is complete. When the horseman succeeds in obtaining it, his talent becomes a truth, since it transforms ugliness into grace, and gives elegance and lightness to movements which were before heavy and confused.*

* I have often proved that horses that were considered dull, or unable to move their shoulders freely, have not

The rider's employment of force, when properly applied, has a moral effect also on the horse, that accelerates the results. If the impulse given by the legs find in the

the defect that is supposed; in other words, that it is very rare that they are paralyzed in their shoulders so as to injure the regularity and speed of their paces, principally as regards trotting. The shoulders of the horse, if I may use the comparison, resemble the wings of a windmill; the impulse given by the hocks replaces the motive force. There undoubtedly exist some local complaints that affect the shoulders; but this difficulty is very rare; the defect, if there be one, has its origin in the hind parts. For my part, I have been able to make all such horses very free in their movements, and that after fifteen days of exercise, half an hour a day. The means, like all I employ, are very simple. They consist in suppling the neck to get the horse in hand, and then, by the aid of the legs, and afterwards slight use of the spurs, in bringing his haunches nearer the centre. Then the hocks will obtain a leverage, by which they can propel the mass forward, and give the shoulders a freedom that people would not expect.

hand the energy and *àpropos* necessary to regulate its effects, the pain which the animal sustains will always be proportioned to his resistances; and his instinct will soon make him understand how he can diminish, and even avoid altogether this constraint, by promptly yielding to what we demand of him. He will hasten then to submit, and will even anticipate our desires. But, I repeat, it is only by means of tact and delicate management that we will gain this important point. If the legs give too vigorous an impulse, the horse will quickly overcome the motion of the hands, and resume with his natural position all the advantages it gives him to foil the efforts of the rider. If, on the contrary, the hand present too great a resistance, the horse will soon overcome the legs, and find a means of defending himself by backing. Yet these difficulties must not be allowed to frighten us; they were only serious ones when no rational principle gave the means of surmounting them. The application of my method will enable ordinary horsemen to obtain results that otherwise could be obtained only by the most favored equestrian organizations.

When the animal becomes accustomed by means of the spur to such oppositions, it will be easy enough to combat with the spur all the resistances that may afterwards manifest themselves. Since the resistances are always caused by moving the croup sideways, or getting it too far back, the spur, by immediately bringing the hind legs towards the centre of the body, prevents the support of the hocks, which opposed the proper harmony of forces, and prevented the right distribution of the weight.

This is the means I always employ to make the horse pass from a swift gallop to a halt, without straining his hocks, or injuring any of the joints of his hind parts. In fact, since it is the hocks which propel the mass forward, destroying their motion suffices to stop the bound. The spur, by instantly bringing the hind legs under the horse's belly, destroys their power from the moment the hand comes, in the nick of time, to fix them in that position. Then the haunches bend, the croup is lowered; the weight and forces arrange themselves in the order most favorable to the free and combined play of each part, and the violence of the shock, infinitely decomposed, is scarce perceptible either to horse or rider.

If, on the contrary, we stop the horse by making the hand move first, the hocks remain far in the rear of the plumb-line; the shock is violent, painful for the animal, and especially injurious to his physical organization. Horses that are thus stopped, set themselves against the bit, extending their neck, and require an arm of iron and a most violent opposing force. Such is the custom of the Arabs, for example, in halting suddenly their horses, by making use of murderous bits that break the bars of their horse's mouths. Thus, notwithstanding the wonderful powers with which nature has gifted them, are these excellent animals injured. The use of the spur must not be commenced till by gathering him we get the horse well in hand; then the first touch of the spur should be given. We will continue to make use of it, at long intervals, until the horse, after his bound forward, presents no resistance to the hand, and avoids the pressure of the bit, by bringing in his chin towards his chest, of his own accord. This submission once obtained, we can undertake the use of the spurs with oppositions, but we must be careful to discontinue them when the horse is in hand. This means has the double advantage of acting morally and physically. The first attacks will be made with a single spur, and by bearing on the opposite rein; these transverse oppositions will have a better effect, and give more prompt results. When the horse begins to contain himself, the two spurs being used separately, we can make them felt together and with an equal gradation.*

* I would never have thought that this means, which serves as a corrective to the processes used by all horsemen, would have aroused the sensibility of some amateurs. These latter have preferred to be affected by exaggerated or erroneous reports, rather than satisfy themselves by observation that this pretended cruelty is in fact the most innocent thing in the world. Must we not teach the horse to respond to the spur as well as to the

To the work, then, cavaliers! If you will follow my principles, I can promise you that your purses will be less often emptied into the hands of horse-dealers, and that you will render the meanest of your hacks agreeable. You will charm our breeders of horses, who will attribute to their efforts of regeneration that elegance and grace which your art alone could have given to your chargers.

Lowering the hand.—The lowering the hand consists in confirming the horse in all his lightness—that is, in making him preserve his equilibrium without the aid of the reins. The suppleness given to all parts of

legs and the hand? Is it not by this spurring, judiciously applied, that we bring in at will the hind legs more or less near the centre of gravity? Is not this the only way of increasing or diminishing the leverage of the hocks, whether for extending or raising them in motion, or for the purpose of halting?

the horse, the just oppositions of hands and legs, lead him to keep himself in the best possible position. To find out exactly whether we are obtaining this result, we must have recourse to frequent lowering of the hand. It is done in this way. After having slipped the right hand to the buckle, and having assured yourself that the reins are even, you will let go of them with the left hand, and lower the right slowly to the pommel of the saddle. To do this regularly, the horse must neither increase nor diminish the speed of his pace, and his head and neck must continue to preserve their proper position. The first few times that the horse is thus given up to himself, he will perhaps only take a few steps while keeping in position, and at the same rate of speed; the rider ought then to make his legs felt first, and the hand afterwards, to bring him into his previous position. The frequent repetition of this lowering of the hand, after a complete placing of the horse's head in a perpendicular position, will give him a most exquisite mouth, and the rider a still greater delicacy of touch. The means of guiding employed by the latter will immediately be answered by the horse, if his forces have been previously disposed in a perfectly harmonious state.

The lowerings of the hand ought to be practised first at a walk, then at a trot, afterwards at a gallop. This semblance of liberty gives such confidence to the horse that he gives up without knowing it; he becomes our submissive slave, while supposing that he is preserving an entire independence.

Of gathering the horse, or rassembler.—The preceding exercise will render easy to the rider that important part of horsemanship called *rassembler*. This has been a great deal talked about by people, as they have talked about Providence, and all the mysteries that are impenetrable to human perception. If it were allowable for us to compare small things with great, we might say that the more or less absurd theories which have been put forward upon the subject of divine power, have not, fortunately, hindered in any way the unchangeable march of nature; but with regard to the progress of horsemanship, the case is not the same, as to what has been said and written on the subject of the *rassembler*. The false principles propagated on this subject have made the horse the plaything and the victim of the rider's ignorance.

I proclaim it, the gathering a horse has never been understood or defined before me, for it cannot be perfectly executed without the regular application of the principles which I have developed for the first time. You will be convinced of this truth when you know that the *rassembler* demands :—

1. The suppling, partial and general, of the neck and haunches.

2. The perfect position that results from this suppling.

3. The entire absorption of the forces of the horse by the rider.

Now, as the means of obtaining these different results have never been pointed out in any treatise on horsemanship, am I not justified in saying that the true *rassembler* has never been practised until now? It is, nevertheless, one of the indispensable conditions of the horse's education; consequently, I think I am right in saying that, before my method, horses of defective formation have never been properly broken.

How is the *rassembler* defined in the

schools of horsemanship? *You gather your horse by raising the hand and closing the legs.* I ask, what good can this movement of the rider do upon an animal badly formed, contracted, and that remains under the influence of all the evil propensities of its nature? This mechanical support of the hands and legs, far from preparing the horse for obedience, will only make him redouble his means of resistance; since, while giving him notice that we are about to demand a movement on his part, we remain unable to dispose his forces in such a way as to force him to it.

The real *rassembler* consists in collecting the forces of the horse in his centre in order to ease his extremities, and give them up completely to the disposition of the rider. The animal thus finds himself transformed into a kind of balance, of which the rider is the centre-piece. The least touch upon one or other of the extremities, which represent the scales, will immediately send them in the direction we wish. The rider will know that his horse is completely gathered when he feels him ready, as it were, to rise from all four of his legs. The proper position first, and then the use of the spurs, will make this beautiful execution of the gathering easy to both horse and rider; and what splendor, grace, and majesty it gives the animal! If we have been obliged at first to use the spurs in pushing this concentration of forces to its farthest limits, the legs will afterwards be sufficient to obtain the gathering necessary for the precision and elevation required in all complicated movements.

Need I recommend discretion in your demands? I think not. If the rider, having reached this stage of his horse's education, cannot comprehend and seize that fineness of touch, that delicacy of process, indispensable to the right application of my principles, it will prove him devoid of every feeling of a horseman; nothing I can say can remedy this imperfection of his nature.

VII.

OF THE EMPLOYMENT OF THE FORCES OF THE HORSE BY THE RIDER.

(*Continuation.*)

Of the gallop.—I have said that, until now, the greater part of the resources of horsemanship have not been understood; and had I need of other proofs to support my opinion, I would draw them from the errors, the suppositions, and the innumerable contradictions, which have been heaped together in order to explain so simple a movement as the gallop. What contrary opinions upon the means to be employed to make the horse go off with his right foot! It is the support of the rider's right leg which determines the movement, one pretends; it is that of the left leg, says another; it is the equal touch of the two legs, affirms a third; no, some others remark, very seriously, you must let the horse act naturally.

How can the truth be made out in the midst of this conflict of such contrary principles? Besides, they come from such respectable sources; the most of their authors were possessed of titles and dignities which are generally only granted to merit. Have they all been deceived for a hundred and fifty years? This is not possible; for many of them joined to long practice a perfect knowledge of physics, anatomy, mathematics, &c. &c. To doubt such authorities would be as presumptuous as imprudent; it would have been considered a crime of high treason against horsemanship. So the riders kept their ignorance, and the horses their bad equilibrium; and if any one succeeded, after two or three years of routine labor, in making certain horses of a privileged organization start with the desired foot, and in making them change feet finally, at a fixed point, the difficulty then was to prevent them from always repeating this movement at the same place.

Thus it is that the most palpable errors gain credit, and often are perpetuated, until there comes a practical mind, gifted with some amount of common sense, who contradicts by practice all the learned theories of its predecessors. They try hard at first to deny the knowledge of the innovator; but the masses, who instinctively know the truth, and judge from what they see, soon range themselves on his side, turn their backs upon his detractors, and leave them to their solitude and vain pretensions.

To the mass of horsemen I address myself, when I say, either the horse is under the influence of your forces, and entirely submissive to your power, or you are struggling with him. If he gallop off with you, without your being able to modify or direct with certainty his course, it proves that, although subject to a certain extent to your power, in thus consenting to carry you about, he nevertheless uses his instinctive forces. In this case, there is a perpetual fight going on between you and him, the chances of which depend on the temperament and caprice of the animal—upon the good or bad state of his digestion. Changes of foot, in such a state, can only be obtained by inclining the horse very much to one side, which makes the movement both difficult and ungraceful.

If, on the contrary, the animal is made submissive to a degree that he cannot contract any one of his parts without the intervention and aid of the rider, the latter can direct at his pleasure the whole of his moving parts, and, consequently, can easily and promptly execute changes of feet.

We know the contraction of any one part of the horse reacts on the neck, and that the stiffness of this part prevents the proper execution of every movement. If, then, at the moment of setting off on a gallop, the horse stiffen one of his extremities, and consequently his neck, of what use, in determining his starting with the right foot, can be the support of one or the other leg of the rider, or even of that of both at once? These means will evidently be ineffectual until we go back to the source of the resistance, for the purpose of combating and destroying it. Here, as in every other case, we see that suppleness and lightness alone can make the execution of the work easy.

If, when we wish to make the horse start with the right foot, a slight contraction of one part of the animal dispose him to start with the left foot, and we persist in inducing the pace, we must employ two forces on the same side, viz., the left leg and the left hand; the first to determine the movement, the second to combat the contrary disposition of the horse.

But when the horse, that is perfectly supple and gathered, only brings his parts into play after the impression given them by the rider, the latter, in order to start with the right foot, ought to combine an opposition of forces proper for keeping the horse in equilibrium, while placing him in the position required for the movement. He will then bear the hand to the left, and press his right leg. Here we see that the means mentioned above, necessary when the horse is not properly placed, would be wrong when the animal is properly placed, since it would destroy the harmony then existing between his forces.

This short explanation will, I hope, suffice to make it understood that things should be studied thoroughly before laying down any principles of action. Let us have no more systems then upon the exclusive use of such or such a leg to determine the gallop; but a settled conviction that the first condition of this, or any other performance, is to keep the horse supple and light —that is *rassemblé;* then, after this, to make use of one or the other motive power, according as the animal, at the start, preserves a proper position, or seeks to leave it. It must also be understood that, while it is the force that gives the position to the horse, it is position alone upon which the regularity of movement depends.

Passing frequently from the gallop with the right foot to that with the left, in a straight line, and with halts, will soon bring the horse to make these changes of feet by the touch, without halting. Violent effects of force should be avoided, for they only bewilder the horse and destroy his lightness. We must remember that this lightness, which should precede all changes of pace and direction, and make every movement easy, graceful, and inevitable, is the important condition we should seek before everything else.

It is because they have not understood this principle, and have not felt that the first condition, to dispose a horse for the gallop, is to destroy all the instinctive forces of the animal (forces that oppose the position the movement demands), that horsemen have laid down so many erroneous principles, and have all remained unable to show us the proper means to be employed.

Of leaping the ditch and the bar.—Although the combinations of equestrian science alone cannot give to every horse the energy and vigor necessary to clear a ditch or a bar, there are, nevertheless, principles by the aid of which we will succeed in partly supplying the deficiencies in the natural formation of the animal. By giving a good direction to the forces, we will facilitate the rise and freedom of the bound. I do not pretend by this to say, that a horse of ordinary capabilities will attain the same height and elegance in this movement as one that is well constituted, but he will, at least, be able to display in it all the resources of his organization to more purpose.

The great thing is to bring the horse to attempt this performance with good will. If all the processes prescribed by me for mastering the instinctive forces of the animal, and putting him under the influence of ours have been punctually followed, the utility of this progression will be recognized by the facility we have of making the horse clear all the objects that are encountered in his way. For the rest, recourse must never be had, in case of a contest, to violent means, such as a whip in the hands of a second person; nor should we seek to excite the animal by cries; this could only produce a moral effect, calculated to frighten him. It is by physical means alone that we should bring him to obedience, since they alone will enable him to understand and execute. We should then carry on the contest calmly, and seek to surmount the forces that lead him to refuse, by acting directly on them. To make the horse leap, we will wait till he responds freely to the legs and spur, in order to have always a sure means of government.

The bar will remain on the ground until the horse goes over it without hesitation;

it will then be raised some inches, progressively increasing the height, until the animal will be just able to clear it without too violent an effort. To exceed this proper limit, would be to risk causing a disgust on the part of the horse that should be most carefully avoided. The bar having been thus gradually raised, ought to be made fast, in order that the horse, disposed to be indolent, should not make sport of an obstacle which would be no longer serious, when the touch of his feet sufficed to overturn it. The bar ought not to be wrapped in any covering that would lessen its hardness; we should be severe when we demand possibilities, and avoid the abuses that always result from an ill-devised complaisance.

Before preparing to take the leap, the rider should hold himself sufficiently firm to prevent his body preceding the motion of the horse. His loins should be supple, his buttocks well fixed to the saddle, so that he may experience no shock nor violent reaction. His thighs and legs exactly enveloping the body and sides of the horse, will give him a power always opportune and infallible. The hand in its natural position will feel the horse's mouth in order to judge of the effects of impulsion. It is in this position that the rider should conduct the horse towards the obstacle; if he come up to it with the same freedom of pace, a light opposition of the legs and hand will facilitate the elevation of the fore-hand, and the bound of the posterior extremity. As soon as the horse is raised, the hand ceases its effect, to be again sustained when the fore-legs touch the ground, so as to prevent them giving way under the weight of the body.

We should content ourselves with executing a few leaps in accordance with the horse's powers, and above all avoid pushing bravado to the point of wishing to force the animal over obstacles that are beyond his powers. I have known very good leapers that people have succeeded in thus disgusting forever, so that no efforts could induce them to clear things only half the height of those that at first they leaped with ease.

*Of the piaffer.**—Until now, horsemen have maintained that the nature of each horse permits of only a limited number of movements, and that, if there are some that can be brought to execute a *piaffer* high and elegant, or low and precipitate, there are a great number of them to whom this exercise is forever interdicted. Their construction, they say, is opposed to it; it is, then, nature that has so willed it; ought we

* "The *piaffer* is the horse's raising his legs diagonally as in the trot, but without advancing or receding."—Baucher's "*Dictionaire d' Equitation.*"

not to bow before this supreme arbiter and respect its decrees?

This opinion is undoubtedly convenient for justifying its own ignorance, but it is none the less false. *We can bring all horses to piaffer;* and I will prove that, in this particularly, without reforming the work of nature, without deranging the formation of the bones, or that of the muscles of the animal, we can remedy the consequences of his physical imperfections, and change the vicious disposition occasioned by faulty construction. There is no doubt that the horse whose forces and weight are collected in one of his extremities will be unfit to execute the elegant cadence of the *piaffer*. But a graduated exercise, the completion of which is the *rassembler*, soon allows us to remedy such an inconvenience. We can now reunite all these forces in their true centre of gravity, and the horse that bears the *rassembler* perfectly has all the necessary qualifications for the *piaffer*.

For the *piaffer* to be regular and graceful, it is necessary that the horse's legs, moved diagonally, rise together, and fall in the same way, upon the ground, at as long intervals as possible. The animal ought not to bear more upon the hand than upon the legs of the rider, that his equilibrium may present the perfection of that balance of which I have spoken in another place. When the centre of the forces is thus disposed in the middle of the body, and when the *rassembler* is perfect, it is sufficient, in order to induce a commencement of *piaffer* to communicate to the horse with the legs a vibration at first slight, but often repeated. By vibration, I mean an invigoration of forces, of which the rider ought always to be the agent.

After this first result, the horse will be

put at a walk, and the rider's legs, gradually brought close, will give the animal a slight increase of action. Then, but only then, the hand will sustain itself in time with the legs, and at the same intervals; in order that these two motive powers, acting conjointly, may keep up a succession of imperceptible movements, and produce a slight contraction which will spread itself over the whole body of the horse. This reiterated activity will give the extremities a motion, which at the beginning will be far from regular, since the increase of action that this new exercise makes necessary will for the moment break the harmonious uniformity of the forces. But this general action is necessary in order to obtain even an irregular mobility; for without it the movement would be disorderly, and there would be a want of harmony among the different springs. We will content ourselves, for the first few days, with a commencement of mobility in the extremities, being careful to stop each time that the horse raises or puts down his feet, without advancing them too much, in order to caress him, and speak to him, and thus calm the invigoration that a demand, the object of which he does not understand, must cause in him. Nevertheless, these caresses should be employed with discernment, and only when the horse has done well; for, if badly applied, they would be rather injurious than useful. The fit time for ceasing with the hands and legs is more important still; it demands all the rider's attention.

The mobility of the legs once obtained, we can commence to regulate it, and fix the intervals of the cadence. Here again, I seek in vain to indicate with the pen the degree of delicacy necessary in the rider's proceedings, since his motions ought to be answered by the horse with an exactness and *à propos* that is unequalled. It is by the alternated support of the two legs that he will succeed in prolonging the lateral balancings of the horse's body, in such way as to keep him longer on one side or the other. He will seize the moment when the horse prepares to rest his fore-leg on the ground, to make the pressure of his own leg felt on the same side, and add to the inclination of the animal in the same direction. If this time is well seized, the horse will balance himself slowly, and the cadence will acquire that elevation so fit to bring out all its elegance and all its majesty. These times of the legs are difficult, and require great practice; but their results are too splendid for the rider not to strive to seize the light variations of them.

The precipitate movement of the rider's legs accelerates also the *piaffer*. It is he, then, who regulates at will the greater or less degree of quickness in the cadence. The performance of the *piaffer* is not elegant and perfect until the horse performs it without repugnance, which will always be the case when the forces are kept together, and the position is suitable to the demands of the movement. It is urgent, then, to be well acquainted with the amount of force necessary for the performance of the *piaffer*, so as not to overdo it. We should above all be careful to keep the horse *rassemblé*, which, of itself, will induce the movement without effort.

VIII.

DIVISION OF THE WORK.

I HAVE developed all the means to be employed in completing the horse's education; it remains for me to say how the horseman should divide his work, in order to connect the different exercises, and pass by degrees from the simple to the more complicated.

Two months of work, consisting of two lessons a day of a half hour each—that is to say, one hundred and twenty lessons, will be amply sufficient to bring the greenest horse to perform regularly all the preceding exercises. I hold that two short lessons a day, one in the morning, the other in the afternoon, are necessary to obtain good results.

We disgust a young horse by keeping

him too long at exercises that fatigue him; the more so as his intelligence is less prepared to understand what we demand of him. On the other hand, an interval of twenty-four hours is too long, in my opinion, for the animal to remember what he may have comprehended the day before.

The general work will be divided into five series or lessons, distributed in the following order:—

First lesson. Eight days of wor.k—The first twenty minutes of this lesson will be devoted to the stationary exercise for the flexions of the jaw and neck; the rider first on foot, and then on horseback, will follow the progression I have previously indicated. During the last ten minutes, he will make the horse go forward at a walk, without trying to animate him, applying himself all the while to keeping the animal's head in the position of *ramener*. He will content himself with executing a single change of hand, in order to go as well to the right hand as to the left. The fourth or fifth day, the rider, before putting his horse in motion, will make him commence some slight flexions of the croup.

Second lesson. Ten days of work.—The first fifteen minutes will be occupied in the stationary supplings, comprising the flexions of the croup, performed more completely than in the preceding lesson; then will begin the backing. We will devote the other half of the lesson to moving straight ahead, once or twice taking the trot at a very moderate pace. The rider during this second part of the work, without ceasing to pay attention to the *ramener*, will commence light oppositions of hand and legs, in order to prepare the horse to bear the combined effects, and to give regularity to his paces. We will also commence the changes of direction at a walk, while preserving the *ramener*, and being careful always to make the head and neck go first.

Third lesson. Twelve days of work.—Six or eight minutes only will at first be occupied in the stationary flexions; those of the hind parts should be pushed to the completion of the reversed *pirouettes.* We will continue by the backing; then all the rest of the lesson will be devoted to perfecting the walk and the trot, commencing at this latter pace the changes of direction. The rider will often stop the horse, and continue to watch attentively the *ramener* during the changes of pace or direction. He will also commence the exercise *de deux pistes* at a walk, as well as the rotation of the shoulders around the haunches.

Fourth lesson. Fifteen days of work.—After five minutes being devoted to the stationary supplings, the rider will first repeat all the work of the preceding lessons; he will commence, with a steady foot, the *attaques*,* in order to confirm the *ramener*, and prepare the *rassembler*. He will renew the *attaques* while in motion, and when the horse bears them patiently, he will commence the gallop. He will content himself in the commencement with executing four or five lopes only, before resuming the walk; and he will then start again with a different foot—unless the horse require being exercised oftener on one foot than the other. In passing from the gallop to the walk, we should watch with care that the horse resumes this latter pace as quickly as possible, without taking short steps on a trot, all the while keeping his head and neck light. He will only be exercised at the gallop at the end of each lesson.

* The use of the spurs.

Fifth lesson. Fifteen days of work.—These last fifteen days will be occupied in assuring the perfect execution of all the preceding work, and in perfecting the pace of the gallop, until we can easily execute changes of direction, changes of feet at every step, and passaging. We may then exercise the horse at leaping the bar, and at the *piaffer*. Thus in two months, and upon any horse, we will have accomplished a work that formerly required years, and then often gave incomplete results. And I repeat, however insufficient so short a space of time may appear, it will produce the effect I promise, if you follow exactly all my directions. I have demonstrated this upon a hundred different occasions, and many of my pupils are able to prove it as well as myself.

In establishing the above order of work, be it well understood, that I base my directions upon the dispositions of horses in general. A horseman of any tact will soon understand the modifications that he ought to make in their application, according to the particular nature of his pupil. Such a horse, for example, will require more or less persistence in the flexions; another one in the backing; this one, dull and apathetic, will require the use of the spurs before the time I have indicated. All this is an affair of intelligence; it would be to insult my readers, not to suppose them capable of supplying to the details what it is impossible to particularize. You can readily understand that there are irritable, ill-disposed horses, whose defective dispositions have been made worse by previous bad management. With such subjects it is necessary to put more persistence into the supplings and the walk. In every case, whatever the slight modifications, that a difference in the dispositions of the subjects render necessary, I persist in saying that there are no horses whose education ought not to be completed, by my method, in the space which I designate. I mean here, that this time is sufficient to give the forces of the horse the fitness necessary for executing all the movements; the finish of education depends finally on the nicety of the rider's touch. In fact, my method has the advantages of recognizing no limits to the progress of equitation; and there is no performance, *equestrianly* possible, that a horseman, who understands properly applying my principles, cannot make his horse execute. I am about to give a convincing proof in support of this assertion, by explaining the sixteen new figures of the *manege* which I have added to the collection of the old masters.

IX.

APPLICATION OF THE PRECEDING PRINCIPLES TO THE PERFORMANCE OF THE HORSES, PARTISAN, CAPITAINE, NEPTUNE, AND BURIDAN.

THE persons who systematically denied the efficacy of my method, should also necessarily deny the results shown to them. They were forced to acknowledge that my performance at the *Cirque-Olympique* was new and extraordinary; but they attributed it to curious causes—some more strange than others; all the while insisting that the equestrian talent of the rider did not go for nothing in the expertness of the horse. According to some, I was a second Carter, accustoming my horses to obedience by depriving them of sleep and food; according to others, I bound their legs with cords, and thus held them suspended, to prepare them for a kind of puppet-show; some were not far from believing that I fascinated them by the power of my looks. Finally, a certain portion of the public, seeing these animals perform in time to the charming music of one of my friends, M. Paul Cuzent, insisted seriously that they undoubtedly possessed, in a very great degree, the instinct of melody, and that they would stop short with the clarionets and trombones. So, the sound of the music was more powerful over my horse than I was myself! The animal obeyed a *do* or a *sol*, nicely touched, but the effects of my legs and hands went for nothing. Would it be believed that such nonsense was uttered by people that passed for riders? I can comprehend their not having understood my means at first, since my method was new; but before judging it in so strange a manner, they ought, at least, it seems to me, to have sought to understand it.

I had found the round of ordinary equestrian feats too limited; since it was sufficient to execute one movement well, to immediately practise the others with the same facility. So, it was proved to me, that the rider who passed with precision along a straight line sideways, (*de deux pistes*) at a walk, trot, and gallop, could go in the same way with the head or the croup to the wall, with the shoulder in, perform the ordinary or reversed volts, the changes and counterchanges of hands, &c. &c. As to the *piaffer*, it was, as I have said, nature alone that settled this. This long and fastidious performance had no other variations than the different titles of the movements, since it was sufficient to vanquish one difficulty to be able to surmount all the others. I then created new figures of the *manège*, the execution of which rendered necessary more suppleness, more *ensemble,* more finish in the education of the horse. This was easy to me, with my system; and to convince my adversaries that there was neither magic nor mystery in my performance at the *Cirque,* I am about to explain by what processes, purely equestrian, and even without having recourse to *piliers,* cavessons, or horsewhips, I have brought my horse to execute the sixteen figures of the *manège* which appear so extraordinary.

1. *Instantaneous flexion and support in the air of either one of the fore legs, while the other three legs remain fixed to the ground.*

The means of making the horse raise one of his fore legs is very simple, as soon as the animal is perfectly supple and *rassemblé.* To make him raise, for example, the right leg, it is sufficient to incline his head slightly to the right, while making the weight of his body fall upon the left side. The rider's legs will be sustained firmly (the left a little more than the right), that the effect of the hand which brings the head to the right should not react upon the weight, and that the forces which serve to fasten to the ground the over-weighted part may give the horse's right leg enough action to make it rise from the ground. By a repetition of this exercise a few times, you will succeed in keeping this leg in the air as long a time as you wish.

2. *Mobility of the haunches, the horse resting on his fore legs, while his hind legs balance themselves alternately, the one over the other: when the hind leg, which is raised from left to right, is moved, and is placed on the ground to become pivot in its turn, the other to be instantly raised and to execute the same movement.*

The simple mobility of the haunches is one of the exercises that I have pointed out for the elementary education of the horse. We can complicate this performance by multiplying the alternate contact of our legs, until we succeed in easily carrying the horse's croup, one leg over the other, in such a way that the movement from left to right, and from right to left, cannot exceed one step. This exercise is good to give great nicety of touch to the rider, and to prepare the horse to respond to the lightest effects.

3. *Passing instantly from the slow piaffer to the precipitate piaffer, and vice versâ.*

After having brought the horse to display great mobility of the legs, we ought to regulate the movement of them. It is by the slow and alternated pressure of his legs that the rider will obtain the slow *piaffer*. He will make it precipitate by multiplying the contact. Both these *piaffers* can be obtained from all horses; but as this is among the great difficulties, perfect tact is indispensable.

4. *To back with an equal elevation of the transverse legs, which leave the ground, and are placed again upon it, at the same time; the horse executing the movement with as much freedom and facility as if he were going forward, and without apparent aid from the rider.*

Backing is not new, but it certainly is new upon the conditions that I lay down. It is only by the aid of a complete suppling and *ramener* that we succeed in so suspending the horse's body that the distribution of the weight is perfectly regular and the extremities acquire energy and activity alike. This movement then becomes as easy and graceful as it is painful, and devoid of elegance, when it is changed into *acculement.*

5. *Simultaneous mobility of the two diagonal legs, the horse stationary. After having raised the two opposite legs, he carries them to the rear and brings them back again to the place they first occupied, and then recommences the same movement with the other diagonal.*

The suppling, and having got the horse in hand, make this movement easy. When he no longer presents any resistance, he appreciates the lightest effects of the rider; which are intended, in this case, to displace only the least possible quantity of forces and weight necessary to set in motion the opposite extremities. By repeating this exercise, it will in a little while be rendered familiar to the horse. The finish of the mechanism will soon give the finish of intelligence.

6. *Trot with a sustained extension; the horse, after having raised his legs, carries them forward, sustaining them an instant in the air before replacing them on the ground.*

The processes that form the basis of my method reproduce themselves in each simple movement, and with still more reason in the complicated ones. If equilibrium is only obtained by lightness, in return, there is no lightness without equilibrium; it is by the union of these two conditions that the horse will acquire the facility of extending his trot to the farthest possible limits, and will completely change his original gait.

7. *Serpentine trot, the horse turning to the right and the left, and returning nearly to his starting point, after having made five or six steps in each direction.*

This movement will present no difficulty if we keep the horse in hand, while executing the flexions of the neck at the walk and trot; you can readily see that such a performance is impossible without this condition. The rider's leg, opposite to the side towards which the neck turns, ought always to be pressed.

8. *Instant halt by the aid of the spurs, the horse being at a gallop.*

When the horse, being perfectly suppled, will properly bear the *attaques* and the *rassembler*, he will be fit to execute the halt upon the above conditions. In the application of this, we will start with a slow gallop, and go on successively to the greatest speed. The legs preceding the hand, will bring the horse's hind legs under the middle of his body, then a prompt effect of the hand, by fixing them in this position, will immediately stop the bound. By this means we spare the horse's organization, which can thus always be kept free from blemish.

9. *Continued mobility or pawing, while stationary, of one of the horse's fore legs; the horse, at the rider's will, executing the movement by which he, of his own accord, often manifests his impatience.*

This movement will be obtained by the same process that serves to keep the horse's leg in the air. In the latter case, the rider's legs must impress a continued support, in order that the force which holds the horse's leg raised keep up its effect; while, for the movement now in question, we must renew the action by a quantity of slight pressures, in order to cause the motion of the leg held up in the air. This extremity of the horse will soon acquire a movement subordinate to that of the rider's legs, and if the time be well seized, it will seem, so to say, that we make the animal move by the aid of mechanical means.

10. *To trot backwards, the horse preserving the same cadence and the same step as in the trot forwards.*

The first condition, in order to obtain the trot backwards, is to keep the horse in a perfect cadence, and as *rassemblé* as possible: the second, is all in the proceedings of the rider. He ought to seek insensibly, by the combined effects, to make the forces of the fore hand exceed those of the hind parts, without affecting the harmony of the movement. Thus we see that by the *rassembler*, we will successively obtain the *piaffer* stationary, and the *piaffer* backwards, even without the aid of the reins.

11. *To gallop backwards, the time being the same as in the ordinary gallop; but the fore legs once raised, in place of coming to the ground, are carried backwards, that the*

hind parts may execute the same backward movement as soon as the fore feet are placed on the ground.

The principle is the same as for the preceding performance; with a perfect *rassembler,* the hind legs will find themselves so brought under the centre, that, by raising the fore hand, the movement of the hocks can only be an upward one. This performance, though easily executed with a powerful horse, ought not to be attempted with one not possessing this quality.

12. *Changing feet every step, each time of the gallop being done on a different leg.*

In order to practise this difficult performance, the horse ought to be accustomed to execute perfectly, and as frequently as possible, changing feet at the touch. Before attempting these changes of feet every step, we should have brought him to execute this movement at every other step. Everything depends upon his aptness, and above all, on the intelligence of the rider; with this latter quality, there is no obstacle that is not to be surmounted. To execute this performance with the desirable degree of precision, the horse should remain light, and preserve the same degree of action; the rider, on his part, should also avoid roughly inclining the horse's fore hand to one side or the other.

13. *Ordinary pirouettes on three legs, the fore leg on the side towards which we are turning remaining in the air during the whole time of the movement.*

Ordinary *pirouettes* should be familiar to a horse broken after my method, and I have above shown the means to make him hold up one of his fore feet. If these two movements are well executed separately, it will be easy to connect them in a single performance. After having disposed the horse for the *pirouette*, we will prepare the mass in such a way as to raise the fore leg; this once in the air, we will throw the weight on the part opposite to the side towards which we wish to turn, by bearing upon this part with the hand and leg. The leg of the rider placed on the converging side, will only act during this time so as to carry the forces forward, in order to prevent the hand producing a retrograde effect.

14. *To back with a halt at each step, the right leg of the horse remaining in front, motionless, and held out at the full distance which the left leg has passed over, and vice versâ.*

This movement depends upon the nicety of touch of the rider, as it results from an effect of forces impossible to specify. Though this performance is not very graceful, the experienced rider will do well to practise it often, in order to learn to modify the effects of forces, and acquire all the niceties of his art in perfection.

15. *Regular piaffer with an instant halt on three legs, the fourth remaining in the air.*

Here, also, as for the ordinary *pirouettes* upon three legs, it is by exercising the *piaffer* and the flexion of one leg separately, that we will succeed in uniting the two movements in one. We will interrupt the *piaffer* by arresting the contraction of three of the legs so as to leave it in one only. It is sufficient, then, in order to accustom the horse to this performance, to stop him while he is *piaffing*, by forcing him to contract one of his legs.

16. *Change of feet every time, at equal intervals, the horse remaining in the same place.*

This movement is obtained by the same proceedings as are employed for changing feet every time while advancing, only it is much more complicated; since we must give an exact impulsion, sufficiently strong to determine the movement of the legs, without the body advancing. This movement consequently demands a great deal of tact on the rider's part, and cannot be practised except upon a perfectly broken horse,—broken as I understand it.

Such is the vocabulary of the new figures of the *manège* which I have created, and have so often executed before the public. As you see, this performance, which appeared so extraordinary that people would not believe that it belonged to equestrianism, becomes very simple and comprehensible, as soon as you have sudied the principles of my method. There is not one of these movements in which is not discovered the application of the precepts which I have developed in this book.

But, I repeat, if I have enriched equitation with a new and interesting work, I do not pretend to have attained the farthest limits of the art; and one may come after me, who, if he will study my system, and practise it with intelligence, will be able to pass me on the course, and add something more to the results which I have obtained.

X.

SUCCINCT EXPOSITION OF THE METHOD BY QUESTIONS AND ANSWERS.

Question. What do you understand by force?

Answer. The motive power which results from muscular contraction.

Q. What do you understand by *instinctive* forces?

A. Those which come from the horse;—that is to say, of which he himself determines the employment.

Q. What do you understand by *transmitted* forces?

A. Those which emanate from the rider, and are immediately appreciated by the horse.

Q. What do you understand by resistances?

A. The forces which the horse presents, and with which he seeks to establish a struggle to his advantage.

Q. Ought we first set to work to annul the forces which the horse presents for resistance, before demanding any other movements from him?

A. Without doubt; for unless we do so, the force of the rider, which should displace the weight of the mass, finding itself absorbed by an equivalent resistance, every movement becomes impossible.

Q. By what means can we combat the resistances?

A. By the methodical and separate suppling of the jaw, the neck, the haunches, and the loins.

Q. What is the use of the flexions of the jaw?

A. As it is upon the lower jaw that the effects of the rider's hand are first felt, these will be null or incomplete if the jaw be contracted or closed against the upper one. Besides, as in this case the displacing of the horse's body is only obtained with difficulty, the movements resulting therefrom will also be painful.

Q. Is it enough that the horse *champ his bit*, during the flexion of the jaw, to leave nothing more to wish for?

A. No, it is also necessary that the horse *let go of the bit;*—that is to say, that he should separate his jaws (at our will) as much as possible.

Q. Can all horses have this mobility of jaw?

A. All, without exception, if we follow the gradation pointed out, and if the rider do not allow himself to be deceived by the flexion of the neck. Useful as this is, it would be insufficient without the play of the jaw.

Q. In the direct flexion of the jaw, ought we to give a tension to the curb-reins and those of the snaffle at the same time ?

A. No, we must use the snaffle first (the hand being placed as indicated in Plate No. 3), until the head and neck are lowered; afterwards the pressure of the bit, in time with the snaffle, will promptly make the jaws open.

Q. Ought we often to repeat this exercise?

A. It should be continued, until the jaws separate by a light pressure of the bit or the snaffle.

Q. Why is the stiffness of the neck so powerful an obstacle to the education of the horse?

A. Because it absorbs, to its profit, the

force which the rider seeks in vain to transmit throughout the whole mass.

Q. Can the haunches be suppled separately?

A. Certainly they can; and this exercise is comprised in what is called stationary exercise.

Q. What is its useful object?

A. To prevent the bad effects resulting from the instinctive forces of the horse, and to make him appreciate the forces transmitted by the rider, without opposing them.

Q. Can the horse execute a movement without a shifting of weight?

A. It is impossible. We must first seek to make the horse take a position which causes such a variation in his equilibrium, that the movement may be a natural consequence.

Q. What do you understand by position?

A. An arrangement of the head, neck, and

body, previously disposed according to the movements of the horse.

Q. In what consists the *ramener?*

A. In the perpendicular position of the head, and the lightness that accompanies it.

Q. What is the distribution of the forces and weight in the *ramener?*

A. The forces and weight are equally distributed through all the mass.

Q. How do we address the intelligence of the horse ?

A. By the position, because it is that which makes the horse understand the rider's intentions.

Q. Why is it necessary that, in the backward movements of the horse, the legs of the rider precede the hand ?

A. Because we must displace the points of support, before placing upon them the mass which they are to sustain.

Q. Is it the rider that determines his horse?

A. No. The rider gives action and position, which are the language; the horse answers this demand, by such a change of pace or direction as the rider intended.

Q. Is it to the rider or to the horse that we ought to impute the fault of bad execution?

A. To the rider, and always to the rider. As it depends upon him to supple and place the horse in the way of the movement; and as, with these two conditions faithfully fulfilled, everything becomes regular, it is therefore to the rider that the merit or blame should belong.

Q. What kind of bit is suitable for a horse?

A. An easy bit.

Q. Why is an easy bit necessary for all horses, whatever may be their resistance?

A. Because the effect of a severe bit is to constrain and surprise a horse, when it should only prevent him from doing wrong, and enable him do well. Now, we cannot obtain these results except by the aid of an easy bit, and above all of a skillful hand; for the bit and the hand are as one, and a good hand is the perfection of a rider.

Q. Are there any other inconveniences connected with the instruments of torture called severe bits?

A. Certainly there are; for the horse soon learns to avoid their painful inflictions, by forcing the rider's legs, the power of which can never be equal to that of a barbarous bit. He succeeds in this by yielding with his body, and resisting with his neck and jaw; so that we miss altogether our proposed aim.

Q. How is it that nearly all the horsemen of renown have invented a particular kind of bit?

A. Because, wanting in personal science, they sought to replace their own insufficiency by aids or strange machines.

Q. Can the horse, perfectly in hand, defend himself?

A. No; for the just distribution of weight, which this position gives, supposes a great regularity of movement, and it would be necessary to overturn this order, before any act of rebellion, on the part of the horse, could take place.

Q. What is the use of the snaffle?

A. The snaffle serves to combat the opposing lateral forces of the neck, and to make the head precede, in all the changes of direction, while the horse is not yet familiarized with the effects of the bit; it serves also to arrange the head and neck in a perfectly straight line.

Q. In order to obtain the *ramener*, should we make the legs precede the hand, or the hand the legs?

A. The hands ought to precede, until they have produced the effect of giving great suppleness to the neck—(this ought to be practised in the stationary exercises); then come the legs, in their turn, to combine the hind and fore parts in the movement. The continual lightness of the horse at all paces will be the result of it.

Q. Ought the legs and the hands to aid one another, or act separately?

A. One of these extremities ought always to have the other for auxiliary.

Q. Ought we to leave the horse a long time at the same pace in order to develop his powers?

A. It is useless, since regularity of movement results from regularity of position. The horse that makes fifty steps at a trot, regularly, is much further advanced in his education than if he made a thousand in a bad position. We must then attend to his position, that is to say his lightness.

Q. In what proportions ought we to use the force of the horse?

A. This cannot be defined, since these forces vary in different subjects; but we should be sparing of them, and not expend them without circumspection, particularly during the course of his education. It is on this account that we must, so to say, create for them a reservoir; that the horse may not absorb them uselessly, and that the rider may make a profitable and more lasting use of them.

Q. What good will result to the horse from this judicious employment of his forces?

A. As we will only make use of forces useful for certain movements, fatigue or exhaustion can only result from the length of time during which the animal will remain at an accelerated pace; and will not be the effect of an excessive muscular contraction, which would preserve its intensity even at a moderate pace.

Q. When should we first undertake to make the horse back?

A. After the suppling of the neck and haunches.

Q. Why should the suppling of the haunches precede that of the loins (the *reculer*)?

A. To keep the horse more easily in a straight line, and to render the flowing, backward and forward, of the weight more easy.

Q. Ought these first retrograde movements of the horse to be prolonged during the first lessons?

A. No. As their only object is to annul

the instinctive forces of the horse, we must wait till he is perfectly in hand, to obtain a backward movement, a true *reculer*.

Q. What constitutes a true *reculer?*

A. The lightness of the horse (head perpendicular), the exact balance of his body, and the equal elevation of the legs diagonally.

Q. At what distance ought the spur to be placed from the horse's flanks before the *attaque* commences?

A. The rowel should not be farther than two inches from the horse's flanks.

Q. How ought the *attaques* to be practiced?

A. They ought to reach the flanks by a movement like the stroke of a lancet, and be taken away as quickly.

Q. Are there circumstances where the *attaque* ought to be practiced, without the aid of the hand?

A. Never; since its only object should be

to give the impulsion which gives the hand an opportunity to contain (*renfermer*) the horse.

Q. Is it the attacks themselves that chastise the horse?

A. No. The chastisement is in the contained position which the *attaques* and the hand compel the horse to assume. As the animal then finds himself in a position where it is impossible to make use of any of his forces, the chastisement has all its efficiency.

Q. In what consists the difference between the *attaques*, practiced after the old principles, and those which the new method prescribes?

A. Our predecessors (whom we should venerate) practiced spurring in order to throw the horse out of himself; the new method makes use of it to contain him within himself—that is, to give him that first position which is the mother of all the others.

Q. What are the functions of the legs during the *attaques?*

A. The legs ought to remain adherent to the horse's flanks, and in no respect to partake of the movements of the feet.

Q. At what moment ought we to commence the *attaques?*

A. When the horse supports peaceably a strong pressure of the legs, without getting out of hand.

Q. Why does a horse, perfectly in hand, bear the spur without becoming excited, and even without sudden movement?

A. Because the skillful hand of the rider, having prevented all displacings of the head, never lets the forces escape outwards, but concentrates them by fixing them within the mass. The equal struggle of the forces, or if you prefer it, their *ensemble,* sufficiently explains the apparent dullness of the horse in this case.

Q. Is it not to be feared that the horse may become insensible to the legs, and lose all that activity necessary for accelerated movements?

A. Although this is the opinion of nearly all the people who talk of this method, without understanding it, there is nothing in what they say. Since all these means serve only to keep the horse in the most perfect equilibrium, promptness of movement ought necessarily to be the result of it; and, consequently, the horse will be disposed to respond to the progressive contact of the legs, when the hand does not oppose it.

Q. How can we judge whether an *attaque* is regular?

A. When, far from making the horse get out of hand, it makes him come in to it.

Q. How ought the hand to be supported,

at moments of resistance on the part of the horse?

A. The hand ought to stop, fix itself, and only be drawn sufficiently towards the body to give the reins a three quarter tension. In the contrary case, we must wait till the horse bears upon the hand, to present this insurmountable barrier to him.

Q. What would be the inconvenience of increasing the pressure of the bit, by drawing the hand towards the body, in order to slacken the horse's paces by getting him in hand?

A. It would not produce an effect upon a particular part, but would act generally upon all the forces, displacing the weight instead of annulling the force of impulsion. We should not wish to unsettle that which we cannot stop.

Q. In what case ought we to make use of the cavesson; and what is its use?

A. We should make use of it if the faulty construction of the horse lead him to defend himself, when only simple movements are demanded of him. It is also useful to use the cavesson with restive horses; as its object is to act upon the moral, while the rider acts upon the physical.

Q. How ought we to make use of the cavesson?

A. At first, the longe of the cavesson should be grasped within fifteen or twenty inches of the horse's head, and it should be held out and supported with a stiff wrist. We must watch the proper times to diminish or increase the bearing of the cavesson upon the horse's nose, so as to use it as an aid. All viciousness is to be repressed by little jerks, which should be given at the very moment of defence. As soon as the rider's movements begin to be appreciated by the horse, the longe of the cavesson should no longer act; and at the end of a few days, the horse will only need the bit, to which he will respond without hesitation.

Q. In what case is the rider less intelligent than the horse?

A. When the latter subjects him to his caprices, and does what he wishes with him.

Q. Are the defences of the horse physical or moral?

A. At first they are physical, but afterwards become moral; the rider ought then to seek out the causes that produce them, and endeavor, by a preparatory exercise, to re-establish the correct equilibrium that bad natural formation prevented.

Q. Can the naturally well-balanced horse defend himself?

A. It would be as difficult for a subject, uniting all that constitutes a good horse, to give himself up to disorderly movements, as it is impossible for the one, that has not received the like gifts from nature, to have regular movements, if art did not lend him its aid.

Q. What do you mean by *rassembler?*

A. The reunion of forces at the centre of gravity.

Q. Can we *rassembler* the horse that does not contain himself under the *attaques?*

A. This is altogether impossible; the legs would be insufficient to counterbalance the effects of the hand.

Q. At what time ought we to *rassembler* the horse?

A. When the *ramener* is complete.

Q. Of what service is the *rassembler?*

A. To obtain without difficulty everything of a complicated nature in horsemanship.

Q. In what does the *piaffer* consist?

A. In the graceful position of the body and the harmonized precision of movements in the legs and feet.

Q. Is there more than one kind of *piaffer?*

A. Two; the slow and the precipitate.

Q. Which is to be preferred of these two?

A. The slow *piaffer,* since it is only when this is obtained that the equilibrium is perfect.

Q. Ought we make a horse *piaffe* that will not bear the *rassembler?*

A. No; for that would be to step out of the logical gradation that alone can give certain results. Besides, the horse that has not been brought forward by this chain of principles, would only execute with trouble and ungracefulness what we ought to accomplish with pleasure and dignity.

Q. Are all riders alike suited to conquer all the difficulties, and seize all the effects of touch?

A. As intelligence is the starting point, for obtaining every result in horsemanship, all things are subordinate to this innate disposition; but every rider will have the power to break his horse to an extent commensurate with his own abilities to instruct.

CONCLUSION.

Everybody complains now-a-days of the degeneration of our breeds of horses. Apprehensive too late of a state of things which threatens even the national independence,* patriotic spirits are seeking to go back to the source of the evil, and are arranging divers systems for remedying it as soon as possible. Among the causes which have contributed the most to the loss of our old breeds, they forget, it seems to me, to mention the decline of horsemanship; nor do they consider that the revival of this art is indispensable in bringing about the regeneration of the horse.

* Much in this chapter, though written for France, applies with great appropriateness to our own country. —Translator.

The difficulties of horsemanship have long been the same; but formerly constant practice, if not taste, kept it up. This stimulant exists no longer. Fifty years ago, every man of rank was expected to be able to handle a horse with skill, and break one if necessary. This study was an indispensable part of the education of young people of family; and as it obliged them to devote two or three years to the rough exercises of the *manège*, in the end, they all became horsemen—some by taste, the rest by habit. These habits once acquired were preserved throughout life; they then felt the necessity of possessing good horses, and being men of fortune spared nothing in getting them. The sale of fine horses thus became easy; all gained by it, the breeder as well as the horse. It is not so now: the aristocracy of fortune, succeeding to that of birth, is very willing to possess the advantages of the latter, but would dispense with the onerous obligations which appertained to an elevated rank. The desire of showing off in public places, or motives still more frivolous, sometimes lead gentlemen of our times to commence the study of horsemanship; but soon wearied of a work without satisfactory results, they find only a monotonous fatigue where they sought a pleasure, and are satisfied that they know enough, as soon as they can stick passably well in the saddle. So insufficient a knowledge of horsemanship, as dangerous as it is thoughtless, must necessarily occasion sad accidents. They then become disgusted with horsemanship and horses; and as nothing obliges them to continue the exercise, they give it up nearly altogether—and so much the more easily, as they naturally care very little about the breeds of horses and their perfection. We must then, as a preliminary measure in the improvement of horses, raise up horsemanship from the low state into which it has fallen. The government can undoubtedly do much here; but it is for the masters of the art to supply, if necessary, what it leaves undone. Let them render attractive, and to the purpose, studies which have hitherto been too monotonous and often barren; let rational and true principles make the scholar see a real progress, and that each of his efforts brings a success with it. We will then soon see young persons of fortune become passionately fond of an exercise, which has been rendered as interesting to them as it is noble; and discover, with their love for horses, a lively solicitude for all that concerns their qualities and education.

But horsemen can aim at still more brilliant results. If they succeed in rendering easy the education of common horses, they will make the study of horsemanship popular among the masses; they will put within reach of moderate fortunes—so numerous in our land of equality—the practice of an art that has hitherto been confined to the rich. Such has been the aim of the labors of my whole life. It is in the hope of attaining this end, that I give to the public the fruit of my long researches.

But I should say, however, that if I was upheld by the hope of being one day useful to my country, it was the army, above all, that occupied my thoughts. Though counting many skillful horsemen in its ranks, the system which they are made to follow—an impotent one in my eyes—is the true cause of the equestrian inferiority of so many, as well as of their horses being so awkward and badly broken. I might add, that to the same motive is to be attributed the little taste for horsemanship felt by the officers and soldiers. How can it be otherwise? The low price allowed by government for horses of remount, causes few horses of good shape to be met with in the army, and it is with such only that education is easy. The officers themselves, mounted upon a very common sort of horses, strive in vain to render them docile and agreeable. After two or three years of fatiguing exercise, they end by gaining a mechanical obedience, but the same resistances and the same faults of construction, are perpetually recurring. Disgusted by difficulties that appear insurmountable, they trouble themselves no more about horses and horsemanship than the demands of the service actually require.

Yet it is indispensable that a cavalry officer be always master of his horse, so much so as to be able, so to say, to communicate his own thoughts to him: the uniformity of manœuvres, the necessities of command, the perils of the battle-field, all demand it imperatively. The life of the rider, every one knows, often depends upon the good or bad disposition of his steed; in the same way, the loss or the gain of a battle often hangs on the degree of precision with which a squadron is manœuvred. My method will give military men a taste for horsemanship, a taste which is indispensable in the profession they practice. The nature of officers' horses, considered as so defective, is exactly the one upon which the most satisfactory results may be obtained. These animals generally possess a certain degree of energy, and as soon as we know how rightly to use their powers, by remedying the physical faults that paralyze them, we will be astonished at the resources which they will exhibit. The rider fashioning the steed, by degrees, will regard him as the work of his hand, will become sincerely attached to him, and will find as much charm in horsemanship as he previously felt *ennui* and disgust. My principles are simple, easy in their application, and within the reach of every mind. They can everywhere make (what is now so rare) skillful horsemen. I am sure that if my method is adopted and well understood in the army, where the daily exercise of the horse is a necessary duty, we will see equestrian capacities spring up among the officers and sub-officers by thousands. There is not one among them who, with the study of an hour a-day, would not be able to give any horse the following qualities and education in less than three months:—

1. General suppling.
2. Perfect lightness.
3. Graceful position.
4. A steady walk.
5. A trot, steady, measured, and extended.
6. Backing, as easily and as freely as going forward.

7. A gallop, easy with either foot, and change of foot by the touch.

8. Easy and regular movement of the haunches, comprising ordinary and reversed *pirouettes*.

9. Leaping the ditch and the bar.

10. *Piaffer*.

11. Halt from the gallop, first by the aid of the pressure of the legs, and then by a light support of the hand. I ask all conscientious men, have they seen many horsemen of renown obtain similar results in so short a time?

The education of the men's horses, being less complicated than that of those intended for officers, would on that account be more rapid. The principal things will be the supplings and the backing, followed by the walk, the trot, and the gallop, while keeping the horse perfectly in hand. The colonels will soon appreciate the excellent results of this exercise, in consequence of the precision with which all the movements are made. The important flexions of the fore hand can be executed, without leaving the stables, by each rider turning his horse round in the stall. It is not for me to point out to the colonels of regiments the exact way of putting my method in practice; it is enough for me to lay down my principles, and to explain them. The instructors will themselves supply the details of application, too long to enumerate here.

I must again repeat that this book is the fruit of twenty years' observation, constantly verified by practice. A long and painful work, without doubt, but such compensation as may be found in the results, I have been happy enough to obtain. In order to let the public judge of the importance of my discoveries, it is sufficient here to give their nomenclature; and I present these processes as new ones, because I can conscientiously say that they never were practiced before me. I have added then successively to the manual of the horseman the following principles and innovations :—

1. New means of obtaining a good seat.

2. Means of making the horse come to the man, and rendering him steady to mount.

3. Distinction between the instinctive forces of the horse and the communicated forces.

4. Explanation of the influence of a bad formation upon the horse's resistances.

5. Effect of bad formations on the neck and croup, the principal focuses of resistance.

6. Means of remedying the faults, or supplings, of the two extremities and the whole of the horse's body.

7. Annihilation of the instinctive forces

of the horse, in order to substitute for them forces transmitted by the rider, and to give ease and beauty of motion to the ungraceful animal.

8. Equal sensibility of mouth in all horses; adoption of a uniform bit.

9. Equal sensibility of the flanks in all horses; means of accustoming them all to bear the spur alike.

10. All horses can place their heads in the position of *ramener* and acquire the same lightness.

11. Means of bringing the centre of gravity in a badly formed horse to the place it occupies in a well-formed one.

12. The rider disposes his horse for a movement, but he does not determine the movement.

13. Why sound horses often are faulty in their paces. Means of remedying this in a few lessons.

14. For changes of direction, the use of the leg opposite to the side towards which we turn, so that it may precede the other one.

15. In all backward movements of the horse, the rider's legs should precede the hands.

16. Distinction between the *reculer* and the *acculement;* the good effect of the former in the horse's education; the bad effects of the latter.

17. The use of the spurs as a means of education.

18. All horses can *piaffer;* means of rendering this movement slow or precipitate.

19. Definition of the true *rassembler;* means of obtaining it; of its usefulness, to produce grace and regularity, in complicated movements.

20. Means of bringing all horses to step out freely at a trot.

21. Rational means of putting a horse at a gallop.

22. Halt at a gallop, the legs or the spur preceding the hand.

23. Force continued in proportion to the forces of the horse; the rider should never yield until after having *annulled* the horse's resistances.

24. Education of the horse in parts, or means of exercising his forces separately.

25. Complete education of horses of ordinary formation in less than three months.

26. Sixteen new figures of the *manège*, proper for giving the finishing touch to the horse's education, and for perfecting the rider's touch.

It is to be understood that all the details of application, appertaining to these innovations, are new, and likewise belong to me.

THE END.

www.ingramcontent.com/pod-product-compliance
Lightning Source LLC
LaVergne TN
LVHW010239110826
845151LV00004B/1343
9781425524081